Best Wishes

Averting the Defense Train Wreck in the New Millennium

D1367378

Significant Issues Series
Timely books presenting current CSIS research and analysis of interest to the academic, business, government, and policy communities.
Managing editor: Roberta L. Howard

The Center for Strategic and International Studies (CSIS), established in 1962, is a private, tax-exempt institution focusing on international public policy issues. Its research is nonpartisan and nonproprietary.

CSIS is dedicated to policy impact. It seeks to inform and shape selected policy decisions in government and the private sector to meet the increasingly complex and difficult global challenges that leaders will confront in the next century. It achieves this mission in four ways: by generating strategic analysis that is anticipatory and interdisciplinary; by convening policymakers and other influential parties to assess key issues; by building structures for policy action; and by developing leaders.

CSIS does not take specific public policy positions. Accordingly, all views, positions, and conclusions expressed in this publication should be understood to be solely those of the authors.

The CSIS Press
Center for Strategic and International Studies
1800 K Street, N.W., Washington, D.C. 20006
Telephone: (202) 887-0200
Fax: (202) 775-3199
E-mail: books@csis.org   Web site: http://www.csis.org/

Averting the Defense Train Wreck in the New Millennium

Daniel Gouré & Jeffrey M. Ranney

Foreword by James R. Schlesinger

Published in Cooperation with Management Support Technology, Inc.

THE CSIS PRESS

Center for Strategic
and International Studies
Washington, D.C.

Significant Issues Series, Volume XXI, Number 6
© 1999 by the Center for Strategic and International Studies
All rights reserved.
Printed on recycled paper in the United States of America

02 01 00 99   4 3 2 1

ISSN 0736-7136
ISBN 0-89206-350-5

Library of Congress Cataloging-in-Publication Data
Gouré, Daniel.
    Averting the defense train wreck in the new millennium / authors, Daniel
Gouré, Jeffrey M. Ranney.
        p.   cm. — (Significant issues series ; v. 21, no. 6)
    ISBN 0-89206-350-5 (alk. paper)
        1. United States — Military policy.   2. United States — Armed
    Forces. I. Title. II. Series. III. Ranney, Jeffrey M.
UA23.G7725   1999
355'.033573 21 — dc21   99-013207
                                                              CIP

Cover design by Robert L. Wiser, Archetype Press, Washington, D.C.

CONTENTS

LIST OF FIGURES

LIST OF TABLES

FOREWORD

James R. Schlesinger

IN JANUARY 1968, PRIME MINISTER HAROLD WILSON ANNOUNCED THAT BRITAIN WOULD WITHDRAW ALL OF HER FORCES "EAST OF SUEZ" BY THE END OF 1971. That hurried withdrawal was the unhappy culmination of a process of strategic realignment forced on the British government more than a decade earlier by burgeoning security commitments and a weak purse. Its immediate cause had been a devaluation of the pound sterling two months before in an effort to stem one of Britain's episodic economic crises. That sent the cost of maintaining Britain's overseas defense commitments soaring. The mismatch between her strategy, forces and resources could only be corrected by a sudden and dramatic retrenchment of Britain's global commitments.

Britain had long known that her defense capabilities and security commitments were out of balance. In fact, the retreat from empire planned by the British government had been far more orderly. This plan would have given Britain's former colonies time to take charge of their own affairs and given the United States the time necessary to avoid a political vacuum in regions of interest to both parties. Instead, an economic crisis had produced a helter-skelter retreat that has resulted in problems for Western security to this day.

Despite the robust condition of the American economy at the end of the twentieth century, we should draw a cautionary lesson from the

---

JAMES R. SCHLESINGER is a former U.S. Secretary of Defense, former U.S. Secretary of Energy, and former Director of Central Intelligence.

experience of what had been the world's greatest empire through the end of World War II. The combination of excessive ambition in foreign affairs, overstretching of the U.S. military, and unwillingness to provide adequate resources to maintain defense capability threatens to confront the United States with precisely the problem faced by Britain 30 years ago. The United States will also face a difficult choice between dramatically higher defense expenditures or a diminished capacity to influence global events—what the authors of this study call a defense train wreck.

No one can foretell what event might precipitate a U.S. defense crisis analogous to London's decision to terminate its tenure as a great power. Already tension exists between surging entitlement spending and the demands of a high-technology military machine for continuous modernization and maintenance. The trend over the past decade to favor the former over the latter has resulted in a U.S. military that has shrunk in size and whose equipment is aging—even as its commitments and overseas deployments have increased. Aging equipment may lead to the failure of a military operation or to the unnecessary loss of human life. Policymakers may become increasingly reluctant to employ military force if there is a significant risk that equipment will not work or there may be significant casualties.

The U.S. military may be approaching a point of no return. The "peace dividend" gained at the end of the Cold War has been spent. The "procurement holiday" we have been on inevitably will come to an end. Virtually the entire stock of military hardware possessed by the armed forces will need to be repurchased over the next 30 years. Yet few in government today are seriously contemplating the level of expenditures that would permit the United States to repurchase the old force, let alone the even greater sums necessary to modernize the force along the lines of the Quadrennial Defense Review (QDR) or acquire a force that integrates the technologies driving the revolution in military affairs (RMA).

The first concrete evidence of the coming defense train wreck can be seen in the operations over Kosovo. The deployment of "an MRC (major regional contingency) worth of air assets" did not substantially damage the world's 35th largest military despite 78 days of continuous bombing. Nor did an MRC worth of air assets overcome the effects of bad weather, terrain, and the adroit management by the Serbian military of its relatively primitive air defense. Yet U.S. forces were stretched to provide the units operating in and around Kosovo. The U.S. Air Force has said that it will need a respite before it can engage in another mini-MRC. Ultimately, Operation Allied Force revealed that Washington has not purchased the capabilities that would allow the U.S. military readily to prosecute one major-theater war, let alone two as outlined in the QDR.

Operation Allied Force also revealed the telltale signs of declining readiness that result from aging hardware, falling personnel retention, and other symptoms of underfunding. If readiness continues to decline, the United States will suffer, in effect, a partial demobilization—and a diminished capacity to shape and influence world events.

U.S. military force structure has shrunk by more than 40 per cent in comparison with that which existed at the end of the Cold War. The smaller force has been stretched thin to meet ambitious foreign policy goals. Over the entire duration of the Cold War, the United States engaged in only 16 smaller-scale contingency operations. Between 1990 and 1997, the U.S. military has conducted 45 such operations. These commitments are increasingly open-ended, requiring a long-term commitment of money, men, and material. The war in Kosovo and the subsequent peacekeeping operation are estimated already to have cost the United States more than $5 billion.

Spreading the burgeoning commitments over a substantially smaller force has accelerated the tempo of operations dramatically. At the end of fiscal year 1998, 26 percent of the total active force was stationed overseas, while more than 50 percent of the navy's surface combatants were deployed around the globe.

This heightened operational tempo reflects an ambitious foreign policy that encourages the belief that the United States will come to the rescue of any beleaguered nation or ethnic minority. Although it is rational that weaker nations around the world should seek to involve the preeminent power in their quarrels, it would not be rational for us to assent to endless open-ended commitments. Although America enjoys great influence and unprecedented prosperity, there are limits and costs to U.S. action.

The coming defense train wreck is principally the result of a failure by the administration to provide the funds necessary to pay for the kinds of military force and tempo of operations dictated by its foreign policy. Despite growing commitments around the world and the proliferation of advanced weapons technologies, the United States has sharply reduced defense spending. The Pentagon has been unable to invest in sufficient training, maintenance, new equipment, and the retention of key personnel to maintain either the technological modernization or the current readiness of the present, reduced force level.

According to Office of Management and Budget projections, defense spending will fall well below the spending requirement to sustain the force outlined in the QDR. Present defense spending is at its lowest level as a percentage of gross domestic product (GDP) since before U.S. entry into World War II. The demobilized United States spent more than 4 percent of its GDP in FY 1941 on defense spending, the year before the Japanese attacked Pearl Harbor. Based on current projections, we will be spending less than 3 per cent of GDP on defense in fiscal year 2000, and even that will decline over the next years.

Averting the Defense Train Wreck in the New Millennium describes the impact on future U.S. military capabilities of persistent underfunding of defense. For more than a decade now, defense budgets have failed to keep up with the needs of the armed forces. If we take depreciation of the existing stock of equipment and the rising price of replacement systems into account, the present shortfall amounts to nearly $100 billion annually. Moreover, underfunding has produced the twin difficulties of a growing backlog of maintenance for existing equipment and a slowdown in the procurement of replacement systems. Continuing on the present course, as the study points out, will result in a U.S. military that is either one-third its present size—but modern—or, should the decision be made to maintain force structure, two-thirds obsolescent.

The United States simply cannot continue to play the global leadership role envisioned by the current national security strategy without a substantial increase in defense spending. The authors conclude that, in the absence of a sizable increase in defense spending, this country will have no other recourse than to significantly retrench its foreign policy commitments and obligations.

We are rapidly running out of time if the nation is to avoid a defense train wreck or an equally significant retrenchment in its foreign policy and relations abroad. Deferring procurement merely creates larger bow waves in the future. It is not possible to wait, as some would suggest, for the so-called revolution in military affairs to reinvent warfare and make existing systems obsolete. If we are to avoid a fate similar to that which befell Great Britain in the early 1970s, we must begin now to achieve a proper balance among international commitments, force levels, and realistic budgets.

PREFACE

Daniel Gouré and Jeffrey M. Ranney

THE UNITED STATES ENTERS THE NEW MILLENNIUM WITH ARGUABLY THE WORLD'S MOST CAPABLE MILITARY. Although it is nearly 40 percent smaller in overall size than at the end of the Cold War, today's U.S. military is capable in principle of the global power projection that is a hallmark of a true superpower. In the 1990s, U.S. military forces enjoyed a number of operational successes and demonstrated a number of astonishing technical achievements—most notably in the Persian Gulf and the Balkans.

Unfortunately, the beginning of the new millennium may well also mark the high point of post–Cold War U.S. military power. For the past decade, the American people have enjoyed a substantial peace dividend in the form of reduced defense spending. There is, however, growing evidence that future budget levels currently projected by Department of Defense (DOD) will not be large enough to pay for maintaining the current planned military force and conducting the range of military activities and operations necessitated by America's national interests and global relationships.

We estimate annual DOD budget shortfalls of nearly $100 billion during the next five years (FY 2001–2005) on the basis of the cost characteristics of the current planned military force and the future defense budget levels currently projected by the Clinton administration, given its long-range vision for the nation and its budget priorities. This situation of underfunding of national defense is not new; it has been going on for some time and will take years to overcome. Military spending is dangerously low in relation to U.S. foreign policy and national security interests—which remain global and immense.

What makes today's situation different is the fact that the equipment of the current U.S. military force is running out of useful life—nearly all at once. Almost 25 years have passed since the start of the most recent DOD procurement modernization cycle. It cannot be stressed enough that the current U.S. military position of unmatched power is a temporary condition: military equipment has a finite life span and, if equipment capabilities are still needed, must eventually be replaced. Strategy, forces, and budgets therefore must finally be reconciled or balanced; if not, military capabilities will be lost forever.

If the current underfunding of national defense is allowed to continue, the United States will face a de facto demobilization and, with it, a diminished capacity to shape and influence world events and to safeguard and protect U.S. national interests in the future. More important, lack of funds will inevitably limit our ability to provide America's soldiers, sailors, and airmen with the pay, support, training and equipment they will require to defeat future adversaries. The consequence could be more than simply a diminution of U.S. influence abroad. The result of underfunding could well be measured in American lives. This outcome we have called a DOD "train wreck."

Consequently, the failure of the Clinton administration and the Congress during 1993–1999 to strike a new balance among strategy, forces, and budgets and the prospects that little will change during the final months of the Clinton administration raise new worries that the defense train wreck might arrive sooner than expected—perhaps sometime during FY 2002–2007. The next elected president (the 43rd president) and Congress (107th Congress) may represent the last chance for finding a way to avert the coming DOD train wreck. Together they will have to make the hard choices that have eluded and escaped the White House, DOD, and Congress in the 1990s. Their failure to do so may result in the train wreck occurring during their terms in office, with lasting political implications.

There has been little public attention or discussion about the fact that DOD is faced with this situation. Today what is needed is a vigorous national debate that addresses the issues of how much it will cost for the

United States to be a great power in the twenty-first century and whether the American people are able and willing to pay those costs. That debate cannot take place unless we are all better informed and realistic about current and future defense costs.

DOD conducted three strategy–budget reviews in the 1990s. All three suffered and lost institutional and public support because of the participants' failure to understand fully and respond to the cost consequences of their decisions and recommendations. The DOD is soon to repeat the mistake as it prepares for its next strategy–budget review in 2001. It is no surprise that the three strategy–budget reviews were driven largely by the politics of defense in terms of shaping and formulating strategy, forces, programs, and budget decisions. At some point, as senior DOD military and civilian officials and Congress are now discovering, fiscal realities must be confronted and resolved.

To strike a balance among strategy, forces, and budgets, the 43rd president and 107th Congress must forge a new consensus and develop an action plan that is realistic about future military requirements and spending demands. As part of this consensus-building process, it is important to recognize and accept the fact that the amount spent on defense will determine the size and the nature of both current and future U.S. military capabilities. Those military capabilities, in turn, will determine the roles the United States can play and the missions it undertakes—and at what risk—in relation to safeguarding and protecting U.S. national interests today and tomorrow. The United States must decide what specific actions to undertake once the Cold War equipment reaches the end of its current operational service life—this is its strategic challenge.

In 1995, in a widely disseminated and well-received Center for Strategic and International Studies (CSIS) report, *Defense in the Late 1990s: Avoiding the Train Wreck,* we warned of a coming defense train wreck that may occur sometime in the FY 2005–2010 period. The warning was issued on the basis of a detailed assessment of the budget demands of the 1993 bottom-up review (BUR) force and the defense budget levels likely to be available in the future as seen in 1993. This book updates and expands in considerable detail those financial analyses and affordability assessments to reflect the recommendations and actions of the 1997

Quadrennial Defense Review (QDR), 1997 National Defense Panel, 1997 secretary of defense's Task Force on Defense Reforms, the president's FY 2000–2005 military spending plan, and congressional actions on the FY 2000 DOD budget. This study was a joint collaborative effort between CSIS and Management Support Technology, Inc. (MSTI). MSTI is located in Fairfax, Virginia, and provides, among other services, strategic planning, defense economics, and budget forecasting services to government and corporate clients.

We initially organized study results into a 50-chart briefing and continuously updated the briefing as events dictated. The purpose of this briefing was to refine the analysis, solicit ideas, and determine effective ways to present the budget data. The briefing was presented many times in 1998 and 1999 to a broad range of individuals and organizations, including former secretaries of defense; senior government executives and flag officers in the offices of the Secretary of Defense, the Joint Chiefs of Staff, and military services responsible for strategic and long-range planning, force planning, and acquisition planning; Congress and congressional committee staff; members of the national press corps, military service associations, and defense industry associations; and senior executives of defense companies.

We observed that in 1995 our analyses and findings were frequently met with much skepticism and outright rejection, especially by senior DOD civilian and military principals. This skepticism gradually faded in 1998. By the fall of 1998 and into 1999, many individuals were expressing concerns and reservations that our analysis and findings were too optimistic as future budget shortfalls were believed now to be larger. Finally, while many have characterized the analysis as pessimistic, gloomy, or overwhelming, we remain optimistic that a solution can be found to avert the DOD train wreck.

We wish to acknowledge the contributions of a number of individuals without whose efforts this endeavor would not have been possible. We are very grateful to the management of both our organizations that enabled this unique collaboration to proceed. Also we would like specifically to acknowledge the ideas, advice, and encouragement of William J. Taylor Jr., Stephen A. Cambone, James T. George, Paul H. Jacobs, and George B. Newton Jr. We are also especially appreciative and grateful to Mary Marik for her skill, patience, and good cheer in preparing the manuscript, tables, and figures. In addition, we wish to thank John Swann and John Mahoney, CSIS International Security Program research associates, for the support they provided. Finally, and most important, we would like to acknowledge the love and support that we have received from our families: Louise and David, and Emilia, Morgan, and Jeffrey.

CHAPTER ONE

INTRODUCTION

In a 1995 report widely disseminated throughout the national security community, analysts at the Center for Strategic and International Studies (CSIS) issued a warning of a coming defense train wreck that would occur sometime in the fiscal year[1] (FY) 2005–2010 period.[2] The warning was issued on the basis of a detailed assessment of the budget demands of the 1993 bottom-up review (BUR) force and the defense budget levels likely to be available in the future.

The 1995 CSIS report defined train wreck:

> The term . . . brings to mind the image of a massive juggernaut racing out of control down the rails until it suffers a catastrophic derailment. Applied to defense in the mid-1990s, the image is one of a downsizing that has become a demobilization without a clearly defined end state.[3]

Today this image still accurately reflects the current state of U.S. military affairs.

There is growing evidence that future budget levels currently projected by the Department of Defense (DOD) might not be large enough to pay for

- developing and acquiring a revolution in military affairs (RMA) force within the next 25 years;
- buying the next generation of military equipment needed to modernize the 1997 quadrennial defense review (QDR) force; or even
- rebuying the current QDR force and military capabilities.

If true, the United States would continue on the present path of a de facto demobilization and, with it, would face a diminished capacity to shape and influence world events and to safeguard and protect U.S. national interests in the future.

The failure of the Clinton administration and the Congress during 1993–1999 to strike a new balance among strategy, forces, and budgets and the prospect that little will change during the final months of the Clinton administration mean future presidents and congresses will have less time to implement solutions and likely will have to pay more for those solutions. Although certainly welcome, President Clinton's February 1999 budget proposal to increase defense spending by $4 billion[4] in FY 2000 and $80 billion during FY 2000–2005 if enacted may be too little, too late.

The inescapable fact is that, in terms of maintaining and sustaining the military capabilities of the QDR force—the desired force for FY 1997–2015—DOD is facing budget shortfalls of at least $100 billion per year instead of in the range of $5–$25 billion per year. Until the White House, DOD, Congress, and the American public recognize and accept the magnitude of this financial problem and undertake specific actions to resolve it, the burden imposed on future presidents, congresses, and the American public will grow heavier.

The absence of any significant progress as the decade of the 1990s comes to a close raises new worries that the defense train wreck may now occur earlier than previously thought—perhaps sometime during FY 2002–2007.

DEFENSE ECONOMICS IS THE NEW THREAT

1997 QDR —
Latest Effort to Reconcile Strategy and Budgets

A major strategic challenge facing today's national security policy-makers and decisionmakers is to create and promote in both the executive and legislative branches a greater awareness and understanding of defense economics. All three defense strategy–budget reviews conducted in the 1990s suffered and lost institutional and public support because senior defense officials failed to understand fully and respond to the cost consequences of their decisions and recommendations. It is no surprise that the three strategy–budget reviews were driven largely by the politics of defense in terms of shaping and formulating strategy, forces, programs, and budget decisions. At some point, as senior DOD military and civilian officials are now discovering, fiscal realities must be confronted and resolved. Their failure to understand fully defense economics contributed significantly to the rapid demise of the 1997 QDR. By late 1998 more and more DOD civilian and military officials began calling for larger budgets.

DOD completed its latest strategy–budget review and its first QDR in May 1997. Secretary of Defense William S. Cohen described the 1997 QDR as the "most fundamental and comprehensive review ever conducted of defense posture, policy and programs."[5] In the *Report of the Quadrennial Defense* Review, he proclaimed the QDR "fiscally responsible" in its view that, barring a major crisis, "the nation is unlikely to support" annual defense budgets in excess of $266 billion.[6] This fiscal reality, he asserted, "did not drive the defense strategy we adopted, but it did affect our choices for its implementation and focused our attention on the need to reform our organization and methods for conducting business."[7] He warned, "it would be unrealistic to build a defense program on an assumption that current resource challenges could be solved by increases in the DOD budget."[8] He concluded with this observation:

> The true test of any financial plan is not only in its numbers, but especially in the stability and reliability of its forecasts and in their suitability to the strategy that they serve. By this measure, the QDR will prove to have made a signal contribution to the Department's stewardship of the resources the nation commits to national defense. While upholding the capability and readiness of the force, the QDR will have launched a plan to modernize for the future whose foundation is more reliable and secure.[9]

The president in February 1998 submitted a DOD budget request of $263 billion for FY 1999. This budget request and accompanying five-year spending plan for FY 1999–2003 reflected for the first time the decisions and recommendations of the 1997 QDR. Later, in October

1998, Congress appropriated $267 billion for FY 1999—$4 billion more than originally requested.

View from the Pentagon

By September 1998, 16 months after the completion of the 1997 QDR, senior DOD military and civilian leaders apparently concluded that the QDR force was not sustainable at projected budget levels. The Joint Chiefs of Staff first advised the president and later disclosed publicly in testimony before the Senate Committee on Armed Services that U.S. military forces are "showing increasing signs of serious wear"[10] and DOD is facing annual budget shortfalls related to military readiness of at least $17.5 billion on a nominal basis[11] starting in FY 2000.

Earlier, in February 1998, as part of his first annual posture statement, chairman of the Joint Chiefs of Staff, General Henry H. Shelton, stated:

> While we are undeniably busier and more fully committed than in the past, the U.S. military remains fully capable of executing the National Military Strategy with an acceptable level of risk. I can assure the Congress that we are not returning to the 1970s. We are fundamentally healthy and continue to report our readiness status to the Congress and American people with candor and accuracy.[12]

In September 1998, however, General Shelton assessed the situation very differently:

> In my view, we have "nosed over" and our readiness is descending. I believe that with the support of the Administration and Congress, we should apply corrective action now. We must "pull back on the stick" and begin to climb before we find ourselves in a nose dive that might cause irreparable damage to this great force we have created, a nose dive that will take years to pull out of.[13]

The chairman's assessment was followed by assessments from each of the service chiefs, who made similar statements and disclosures of declines over the "past several years" in their service's military readiness indicators and provided current estimates of their service's budget shortfalls.

Despite concerns about military readiness, the joint chiefs further testified that their top budget priority, however, was to obtain better military pay and retirement benefits as part of efforts to improve military recruitment and retention rates. They estimated they would need another $6–$7 billion annually on a nominal basis to close the pay gap between military and civilian personnel and to restore the 50 percent pension rate in the military retirement program. As a result of these two budget issues, the joint chiefs reasoned that the DOD budget would have to grow in FY 2000 by $24 billion or 9 percent, from $264 billion (proposed in February 1998) to $288 billion on a nominal basis.

This change in financial outlook was not limited to senior military leaders. In August 1998, in his address to the final meeting of the 1998 Defense Science Board Summer Study, Under Secretary of Defense for Acquisition and Technology Jacques S. Gansler expressed his concerns:

> We are trapped in a "death spiral." The requirement to maintain our aging equipment is costing us more each year: in repair costs, down time, and maintenance tempo. But we must keep this equipment in repair to maintain readiness. It drains our resources—resources we should be applying to modernization of the traditional systems and development and deployment of the new systems. So, we stretch out our replacement schedules to ridiculous lengths and reduce the quantities of the new equipment we purchase—raising their costs and still further delaying modernization. Compounding this problem is the increased operational tempo required by our worldwide role as the sole remaining superpower, which more rapidly wears out the old equipment. And, if this weren't bad enough, we must deal with the uncertainty of unanticipated crises such as the Y2K computer problem, which—in a flat-budget environment—further drain funds from modernization.[14]

The sudden appearance of substantial budget shortfalls and declines in military readiness is difficult to understand, especially before the war in Kosovo, because

- no new or large military threat has emerged since May 1997;
- no significant changes have been made in the size and character of

continuing military operations in Bosnia and the Persian Gulf since May 1997;[15] and

- Congress has approved a defense budget that is $4 billion higher than initially requested by the president.

According to General Shelton, the budget shortfalls and declines in military readiness were the result of several "unanticipated factors" that emerged since the completion of the 1997 QDR:

- U.S. military forces are "far busier" with continuing operations in Bosnia, Haiti, and the Persian Gulf and conducting noncombatant evacuations in Albania and Africa.
- Military departments are experiencing higher-than-anticipated wear on military equipment coupled with rising costs of repair owing to fewer sources of supply.[16]
- Programmed unit, personnel, and base reductions and privatization initiatives are not being carried out as planned.[17]
- Congress "moved some things forward and added some items that were not requested. This altered the delicate balance and created shortfalls in other areas that caused problems for us."[18]
- Recruiting and retention rates are declining because of a continuing strong economy.

View from the Congress

Senator John McCain, a senior member of the Senate Committee on Armed Services, in late September 1998 offered a different explanation in a speech on the floor of the U.S. Senate: "[O]ur armed forces are experiencing problems—problems across the spectrum of readiness, simply because of a chronic tendency by this administration to underfund and overutilize the military."[19] In an earlier speech, McCain stated:

The repeated and deliberate failure to match requirements, as set forth by the National Command Authorities, with resources adequate to the task, compounded by the White House's unwillingness to budget for on-going contingency, peacekeeping and humanitarian operations, has over time, clearly degraded the military preparedness.[20]

In response to concerns about military readiness, Congress approved in October 1998 another $9 billion in so-called emergency funding for military readiness, bringing the total FY 1999 DOD budget to $276 billion. In May 1999, Congress enacted a second emergency supplemental for FY 1999 (PL 106-31) that provided $6.5 billion in funding to finance unbudgeted personnel, operations, equipment replacement, and drawdown costs associated with military operations in Iraq and Kosovo and $3.2 billion to address "existing and urgent shortfalls" in readiness categories.[21] Together, the two emergency funding supplementals brought the total appropriated FY 1999 DOD budget to $286 billion—nearly $20 billion higher ($14 billion excluding the costs of military operations in Iraq and Kosovo) than the May 1997 QDR projection of $266 billion.

Response from the White House

On January 2, 1999, President Clinton announced his decision to submit an FY 2000 defense budget that contained a $12.6 billion (in nominal dollars) increase in FY 2000 and a $112 billion (in nominal dollars) total increase over the six years of FY 2000–2005. If enacted, this will represent the first sustained, long-term increase in defense funding since the end of the Cold War. The president's budget proposal also provided for significant increases in military pay (the largest since FY 1982) and improvements in the military retirement system; the proposal also requested authority for two additional base closure rounds in FY 2001 and FY 2005.

Specifically, the president's military spending plan for FY 2000–2005 proposed to add:

- $35 billion for military pay raises (4.4 percent pay raise in 2000 and 3.9 percent pay raises each year thereafter), including targeted pay raises against certain grades and improvements in retirement benefits, especially the restoration of the 50-percent-of-base-pay formula for calculating retirement pay;
- $10 billion for civilian pay raises (identical to military pay raises);
- $39 billion for Bosnia costs and military readiness enhancements (operations, training, repair parts, and maintenance); and

- $28 billion for defense acquisition programs, to include attainment of the $60 billion annual procurement goal in FY 2001 and procurement funding for national missile defense.

In terms of FY 2000, the president's proposal to increase DOD spending by $12.6 billion consisted of

- $4.1 billion in new budget authority to be allocated from the projected federal budget surplus for that year;
- $3.8 billion in retained savings from lower inflation, foreign currency rates, and fuel prices;
- $3.1 billion in savings attributed to funding incrementally the defense military construction program; and
- $1.6 billion of non-program-specific general reductions.

When viewed from conventional or long-standing, established government budget practices, only $4.1 billion of the president's $12.6 billion increase represented a nominal-dollar increase from the 1999 DOD military spending plan. In real (FY 2000) dollars, it represented a 2 percent decline in spending year-over-year, from $276 billion in FY 1999 (before the enactment of the second emergency supplemental in May 1999) to $270 billion in FY 2000. This conclusion also was reached by the Congressional Budget Office (CBO) and many members of Congress.[22]

For FY 2000–2005, the president planned to finance the defense budget increase by proposing that

- DOD retain $28 billion in savings from the prior year defense budget topline because of revised lower estimates of inflation and fuel prices;[23] rescissions; savings from two additional base closure rounds; savings from future business and energy efficiencies; and non-program-specific general reductions in FY 2000; and
- Congress allocate to defense $84 billion of the projected federal budget surplus once a resolution on Social Security is achieved.

Consequently, only $84 billion (75 percent) of the $112 billion (nominal dollars) budget increase constituted real increases in the defense topline—and only by spending the federal budget surplus.

Measured in terms of FY 2000 dollars, the president's budget proposal adds $80 billion during the next six years to the DOD topline of the previous year. It also is important to emphasize that most of the proposed defense budget increase will occur after President Clinton departs office. It therefore will fall to the 43rd president and the 107th Congress to determine how to pay for the Clinton defense buildup begun in 1999.

Finally, President Clinton, apparently accepting the need for higher defense budgets, at the same time set as a precondition for higher defense budgets that Congress in turn accept his proposals for Social Security reform and for spending the growing federal budget surplus for FY 2000–2009. The president's FY 2000 budget proposal offered this warning: "If Social Security reform is not enacted, discretionary spending levels [for defense] would be reduced to those assumed in the Balanced Budget Act of 1997 for 2001 through 2004."[24]

The effect of this action would be to continue the reductions in defense spending, which the staff of the Senate Committee on the Budget estimated would equal $39.1 billion (nominal dollars) during FY 2000–2003 (the years covered by the Balanced Budget Act of 1997).[25] Moreover, enactment of military and civilian pay raises and improvements in the military retirement system now mean that any future budget cuts will have to be borne entirely by the DOD acquisition (research, development, test, and evaluation [RDT&E] and procurement) accounts. This in turn will place at risk future modernization plans of the military services.

We conclude that, because greater consideration was not afforded to the economics of defense, the 1997 QDR, first, failed to recognize that the demand for future defense spending would exceed $266 billion annually and, second, failed to make the hard program choices necessitated by a decision to limit defense spending to below $266 billion annually.

QDR FORCE NOT ADEQUATELY FUNDED

Unlike the Clinton administration, we believe that the current QDR force, like the BUR force before it, is simply not affordable at the budget levels projected by the DOD over the next 20 years (FY 2001–2020). We

Estimating Future DOD Costs

Estimates of future DOD costs were developed on the basis of a bottom-up budget forecast model that projects the funding needed to maintain a constant force and a constant modernization condition for a postulated force, capability, or activity level.

The budget forecast model draws upon, revises, and updates a budget planning formula first published in *International Security*[1] in 1993 and later used in CSIS's *Defense in the 1990s: Avoiding the Train Wreck* in 1995.[2] The model projects the funding needed over a period of time to provide for steady and continued

- replacement and modernization of military equipment;
- maintenance and support of that equipment;
- manpower acquisition and training of military and civilian personnel in the use and support of that military equipment; and
- payment of salaries and wages, bonuses, allowances, and benefits (retirement, subsistence, housing, medical care, education) of all military and civilian personnel.

The budget forecast model relies on and reflects the interaction of actual historically derived cost trend series related to five major financial measures:

- Operations and support cost trends;
- Military equipment replacement value;
- Military equipment depreciation costs;
- Generational new-procurement unit-cost trends; and
- Procurement according to research, development, test, and evaluation spending (RDT&E) ratios.

Cost trend series were derived from DOD experience during FY 1945–1999, a 54-year period. Despite the end of the Cold War, many of these cost trends continue today. They serve as valid and useful benchmarks for use in assessments of the financial condition and risks associated with current or alternative defense strategies, forces, and budgets.

Notes

1 Dov S. Zakheim and Jeffrey M. Ranney, "Matching Defense Strategies to Resources: Challenges for the Clinton Administration," *International Security* 18, no. 1 (Summer 1993): 51–78.

2 Snider et al., *Defense in the Late 1990s.*

Figure 1.1
DOD Demand for Money in Support of QDR Force, FY 1978–2020

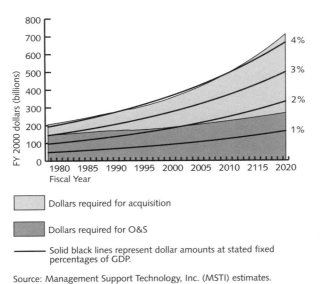

Source: Management Support Technology, Inc. (MSTI) estimates.

reach this conclusion by comparing the funding needed to support fully the QDR force (demand for funds) with the funding that will be available (supply of funds) during the same period.

From the demand perspective (see figure 1.1), the cost of fully supporting the QDR force is estimated to equal 3.9 percent of U.S. gross domestic product (GDP) in FY 2001. Thereafter, to provide for continued modernization and replacement of military hardware, the QDR force will require slightly larger defense budgets. Based on the cost characteristics of the QDR force, the DOD budget will need to equal 4.0 percent of GDP in FY 2010 and, later, 4.3 percent of GDP in FY 2020.

From the supply perspective (see figure 1.2), the February 1999 Office of Management and Budget (OMB) FY 2000–2009 10-year budget projection provided to the Senate Committee on the Budget projected that the DOD budget will grow during this period at an average annual rate of 1 percent, from $270 billion in FY 2000 to $293 billion in FY 2009.[26] Measured in terms of GDP, the DOD budget will fall from 2.9 percent of GDP in FY 2000 to 2.4 percent of GDP in FY 2009. Thereafter,

Figure 1.2
DOD Supply of Money, FY 1978–2020

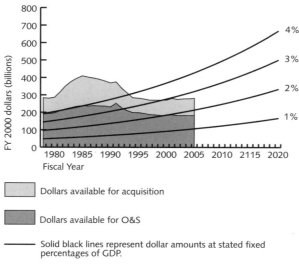

Dollars available for acquisition

Dollars available for O&S

Solid black lines represent dollar amounts at stated fixed percentages of GDP.

Source: MSTI estimates.

if DOD budget levels continue to grow at an annual rate of 1 percent during FY 2010–2020, the DOD budget share will gradually fall from 2.4 percent of GDP in FY 2010 to 2.0 percent of GDP in FY 2020.

A comparison of the demand for funding with the supply of funding (see figure 1.3) indicates that the annual budget shortfall will equal 0.9 percent of GDP in FY 2001. The annual budget shortfall will grow to equal 1.6 percent of GDP by FY 2010 and 2.3 percent of GDP by FY 2020. Furthermore, a DOD budget based on 1 percent growth will equal $327 billion in FY 2020 and will pay for only 46 percent of the costs of the QDR force by FY 2020. The QDR force is therefore not affordable over the long term.

In dollar terms, as illustrated in figure 1.4, it is estimated that a defense budget of $368 billion (the total of the required funding amounts for the four categories in the figure) will be required in FY 2001 to fully support the QDR force. This is $88 billion higher than the $280 billion budget level proposed in the February 1999 DOD spending plan for FY 2001. It represents a budget shortfall of 24 percent.

Figure 1.3
DOD Money, Supply and Demand Balance, FY 1978–2020

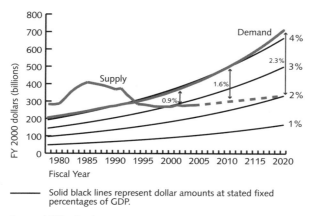

Source: MSTI estimates.

As shown in figure 1.5, the budget shortfall (total dollars required compared with total dollars budgeted) for FY 2001–2005 is estimated to be $573 billion, or 29 percent. This five-year shortfall is equivalent to almost a year and a half of annual DOD funding. That is, the president's DOD spending plan for FY 2000–2005 provided only enough financial resources to pay for three and a half years of the next five years of costs for fully supporting the QDR force.

DOD currently plans to weather this budget shortfall largely by postponing or deferring spending in the DOD acquisition accounts. The acquisition budget shortfall is estimated to be $475 billion and is expected to account for 86 percent of the overall $573 billion budget shortfall for FY 2001–2005. DOD plans during this period to keep low both the number of production lines and annual production rates—well below those levels needed to sustain the QDR force. These actions will lead to further graying (aging) of the QDR force because only minor changes to force structure and equipment inventory levels are expected during this period. Senior defense officials consider this to be an acceptable risk on the basis of their overly optimistic expectations about the capabilities, costs, and schedules of future defense acquisition programs.

Figure 1.4
Potential Budget Shortfall, Dollars Available vs. Dollars Required,
FY 2001

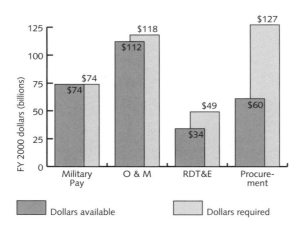

Source: MSTI estimates.

The budget shortfall for DOD military pay and operation and maintenance (O&M) is estimated to be $5 billion and $74 billion, respectively, during the FY 2001–2005. On a nominal basis, the military pay and O&M budget shortfalls are estimated to be $6 billion and $82 billion, respectively. In contrast, after taking the president's proposed budget increase into account, the joint chiefs reported to Congress in February 1999 that budget shortfalls of $37 billion on a nominal basis for unfunded priorities related to military readiness still remain for this same period.[27] Chairman of the Joint Chiefs of Staff Gen. Henry H. Shelton testified before the Senate Armed Services Committee on January 5, 1999: "[A]lthough the President's proposed budget will not satisfy *all* the requirements of the Chiefs identified last year, it *will meet* our most *critical* needs and it *will represent* a major turnaround following years of decreasing spending on defense."[28]

In addition to the budget shortfalls identified by the joint chiefs, DOD projects that on October 1, 2000, depot maintenance backlog will be $1.1 billion (nominal dollars);[29] backlog of maintenance and repair of facilities will be $9.6 billion (nominal dollars);[30] and the army estimates $12 billion (nominal dollars) will be needed to improve condi-

Figure 1.5
Potential Budget Shortfall, Dollars Available vs. Dollars Required,
FY 2001–2005

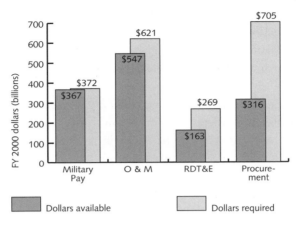

Source: MSTI estimates.

tions at active army facilities to C-1 status (with quality, full mission-ready facilities).[31] Together, these three areas total $23 billion in unfunded requirements at the beginning of FY 2001. Moreover, maintenance requirements are growing faster than maintenance budgets as the force and supporting infrastructure grow older. Similar conditions—expenses exceeding budgets—exist in other categories in O&M accounts.

A substantial defense strategy–resources mismatch therefore already exists. It is profound. It has been ongoing for some time and will take years to overcome. It is reaching crisis proportions and requires immediate attention, involvement, and action by the White House, DOD, Congress, and the general public. It is of great national importance today because military spending levels now are too dangerously low in relation to current and future U.S. foreign policy and national security interests—which remain global and immense.

The issue of affordability is not unique to the QDR force, to the Clinton administration, or to the post–Cold War period. Past U.S. administrations faced similar affordability questions and issues. The decision made in the past too often was simply a decision to defer action and leave it to future administrations to find ways to resolve such budget liabilities. What makes the affordability issue today different is the fact that the current QDR force is running out of useful life—nearly all at once. Almost 25 years have passed since the start of the most recent DOD procurement modernization cycle. It is no longer possible to continue to defer action. Strategy, forces, and budgets must finally be reconciled and balanced; if not, military capabilities will be lost forever.

To strike such a balance, the White House, DOD, and Congress must forge a new consensus and develop an action plan that is realistic about future military requirements and spending demands. As part of this consensus-building process, it is important to recognize and accept the fact that the amount spent on defense will determine the size and the nature of both current and future U.S. military capabilities. Those military capabilities, in turn, will determine the roles and missions the United States can play—and with what risk—in relation to safeguarding and protecting U.S. national interests today and tomorrow.

Congress and the American people must also not forget that the United States is unmatched in military power today and in the foreseeable future because of two historical reasons. First, the forces and military technologies the United States relies on and uses to define its superpower status today—long-range strategic bombers, large composite fighter wings, aircraft carrier battle groups, amphibious readiness groups, nuclear-powered submarines, heavy armored and mechanized divisions, global reach airlift and sealift—are the direct result of higher military spending levels incurred during the Cold War. These military assets are the legacy of the Cold War. They are the results of past investment decisions and spending sacrifices. Second, there are no peer competitors today or in the foreseeable future because no nation was willing, or possessed the means, to spend anywhere near the levels spent by the United States on military capabilities during the past 25 years. It cannot be stressed enough that the current U.S. military position of unmatched power is, however, a temporary condition: the hardware that comprises the military forces has a finite life span and, if hardware capabilities are still needed, must eventually be replaced.

Today the strategic challenge for the United States is to decide which specific actions to undertake once the Cold War equipment reaches the end of its current operational service life. Relative to other nations, it is not known today how much and on what the United States will have to spend to remain unmatched in military power. What is known today is that the relative military spending margin between the United States and other nations already has become considerably smaller, especially in terms of military equipment purchases. If this trend continues, it will raise new concerns and worries about strategies and programs that will be needed in the future to avoid technological surprise, to hedge against potential threats, and, most important, to ensure that the right stuff is acquired and fielded for the threats that will in fact emerge in the future. These decisions will grow in importance, especially at the expected lower budget levels and smaller spending margins.

THE 43rd PRESIDENT AND THE 107th CONGRESS FACE A CRISIS

The significance of an early arrival of the DOD train wreck is alarming and most worrisome. In January 2001 the 43rd president and the 107th Congress will be sworn into office. Shortly after taking office, the newly elected president will submit a defense budget for FY 2002. The 107th Congress later will authorize and approve a defense budget for FY 2002. Together, the 43rd president and the 107th Congress may represent the last chance for finding a way to avert the coming DOD train wreck. Their failure to do so may result in the train wreck occurring during their terms in office. Such an event would have lasting political implications regardless of the exact origins or causes of the train wreck.

It appears today that, regarding the development and use of U.S. military forces, five major defense issues will likely dominate deliberations and actions after the election of 2000:

- A military force that is running out of useful life and requires replacement;
- Defense budgets that continue to fall rather than remain constant and, thereby, require additional cuts in forces, personnel, activity levels, and costs;
- A substantial defense strategy–resources mismatch in which projected DOD budget levels are estimated to be already 30 percent below the costs for maintaining and sustaining the military force;

- Implementation timelines that are too short for alternative defense programs to deliver new capabilities before old capabilities are totally exhausted; and
- A decline in the willingness of political or military leaders to consider or to use military force as concerns arise about the effectiveness of a smaller and older force.

The specific form that the train wreck may take is uncertain. It may be a single event or a chain of events over a short period of time. There are several possibilities. A military operation may fail because of equipment failure due to aging parts. There may be unnecessary loss of human life in another military operation owing to performance degradations. Willingness to use military force may decline because political and military leaders grow reluctant to recommend it or feel less confident that military objectives can be attained successfully, given the declining state of military hardware, material readiness, and personnel readiness. Finally, the DOD train wreck may take the form of changes in global perceptions. Potential adversaries may perceive diminished U.S. military power and seek to exploit perceived weaknesses. Allies may question the credibility of U.S. commitments and seek new reassurances or different arrangements regarding the conduct of U.S. foreign and military affairs.

The year 2001 is emerging therefore as a historic opportunity. The 43rd president and 107th Congress represent one of the last opportunities for defining what kind of military forces and capabilities the United States will have by FY 2010 and what the possibilities are for the second decade of the next century. The 43rd president and 107th Congress unfortunately will have little opportunity to defer or postpone decisions. They will have to make the hard choices that have eluded and escaped the White House, DOD, and Congress in the 1990s. The hard choices are made even more difficult because the actionable time is running out for most DOD program options in terms of defining FY 2010 force capabilities. Implementation timelines are already lengthy, as presented in table 1.1. Today these timelines are becoming longer.

It is not certain how much time the 43rd president and 107th Congress will have before they must act and under what conditions (crisis or noncrisis) or circumstances (single event, series of events, or multiple

Table 1.1
DOD Implementation Timelines

Actions and Processes	Time* (years)
Weapon System Acquisition (time from commencement of the process to fielding of new weapon system)	
Demonstration of advanced technology	8–10
Engineering and manufacturing	5–7
Production	3–7
Manpower Acquisition (time from recruitment to unit assignment)	
Junior officer	5–6
Enlisted person	1–2
Base Closure (time from identification of base to closure)	2–7
Force Reductions (time from decision to implementation)	2–4
Personnel Reductions (time from decision to implementation)	<1

Source: MSTI estimates based on data from DOD.

* Times are not cumulative.

events). What is certain today is the challenges they will face were not made any easier by the failure to act boldly and decisively in the 1990s. It is a real possibility that the 43rd president and 107th Congress may look back on the 1990s as a decade of missed opportunities in a time of ideal international, military, and financial conditions.

ORGANIZATION

This book is organized into six chapters. Following this introduction, chapter 2 describes six dominant attitudes within the national defense establishment—legacies of the 1990s and the Clinton administration—that likely will shape and influence the beliefs, perceptions, and decisions of the next president and 107th Congress during their tenures. Chapter 3 describes in financial terms DOD's current path or direction. It presents and discusses historical and future budget trends that are shaping and influencing the supply of money and the demand for money relating to national defense. Chapter 4 presents and discusses a set of budget projections and affordability assessments for the FY 2001–2010 10-year period in terms of overall DOD, aviation, naval, and army ground combat forces. Chapter 5 identifies and discusses key decisions that the 43rd president and 107th Congress upon assuming office will have to make quickly and early. The sixth and final chapter summarizes major conclusions.

Notes

1 The U.S. government fiscal year runs from October 1 to September 30; for example, FY 2000 begins on October 1, 1999, and ends on September 30, 2000.

2 Don M. Snider, Daniel Gouré, and Stephen A. Cambone, *Defense in the Late 1990s: Avoiding the Train Wreck* (Washington, D.C.: CSIS, 1995). Jeffrey M. Ranney was a principal contributor to this study.

3 Ibid., 8.

4 Unless otherwise stated, all budget figures are reported in constant FY 2000 total obligational authority (TOA) dollars.

5 William S. Cohen, *Annual Report to the President and the Congress* (Washington, D.C.: GPO, 1998), vii.

6 This represents the $250 billion budget level in constant FY 1997 dollars used by the 1997 QDR expressed now in constant FY 2000 dollars.

7 William S. Cohen, *Report of the Quadrennial Defense Review* (Washington, D.C.: Department of Defense, May 1997), v <http://www.defenselink.mil/pubs/qdr/>.

8 Ibid., 19.

9 Ibid., 63.

10 Henry H. Shelton, "Statement of General Henry H. Shelton, Chairman of the Joint Chiefs of Staff, before the Senate Armed Services Committee," September 29, 1998, p. 1 <http://www.dtic.mil/jcs/chairman/SASC29Sept.html>.

11 Nominal dollars represent the current dollar value. No attempt has been made to adjust for the effects of inflation.

12 Henry H. Shelton, "Posture Statement by General Henry H. Shelton, Chairman of the Joint Chiefs of Staff, before the 105th Congress, Senate

Armed Services Committee," February 3, 1998, p. 11.

13 Shelton, "Statement of General Henry H. Shelton," September 29, 1998, p. 5.

14 Jacques S. Gansler, "Remarks at the Defense Science Board: Summer Study Outbrief," August 13, 1998, p. 3.

15 One possible exception is the stationing of two carrier battle groups in the Arabian Gulf for most of FY 1998; however, the additional incremental cost has yet to be disclosed publicly by the navy.

16 For example, in 1998 the commandant of the Marine Corps, General Charles C. Krulak, testified that the cost of an equipment repair order for an average operational unit had increased by 104 percent—from $92 in FY 1995 to $188 in FY 1998—and was projected to continue to climb. See Charles C. Krulak, "Statement of General Charles C. Krulak, Commandant of the Marine Corps, United States Marine Corps, before the Senate Armed Services Committee," September 29, 1998, p. 5.

17 The General Accounting Office (GAO), for example, reported DOD liquidated in 1997 $7.8 billion in operation and maintenance (O&M) reserve funds and $19.8 billion in procurement reserve funds set aside and established in anticipation of savings to be accrued from management initiatives during the FY 1999–2003 period. See GAO, *Future Years Defense Program, Substantial Risks Remain in DOD's 1999–2003 Plan*, GAO/NSIAD-98-204 (Washington, D.C.: GPO, July 1998), 7–10.

18 Deputy Secretary of Defense John Hamre identified $2.1 billion in congressional add-ons to the FY 1999 DOD research, development, test, and evaluation (RDT&E) and procurement authorization bill. See John J. Hamre, "Letter to Senator Carl Levin, September 29, 1998" in *Inside the Pentagon* 14, no. 39 (October 1, 1998): 20–27.

19 John McCain, "Status of U.S. Military Forces and Their Ability to Execute the National Military Strategy," September 29, 1998, in John McCain, *Going Hollow: America's Military Returns to the 1970s, An Update* (Washington, D.C.: Office of Senator John McCain, October 1998).

20 John McCain, "Status of Operational Readiness of U.S. Military Forces," September 10, 1998, in McCain, *Going Hollow*.

21 PL 106-31 also appropriated $1.8 billion for military personnel accounts in FY 2000 to finance increases in military pay, targeted pay increases against certain grades, and reform of the military retirement system.

22 CBO, *An Analysis of the President's Budgetary Proposals for Fiscal Year 2000* (Washington, D.C.: Congressional Budget Office, April 1999), 43–45.

23 For example, DOD assumes the annual inflation rate for defense purchases will remain below 2.1 percent.

24 Office of Management and Budget (OMB), *Budget of the United States Government, Analytical Perspectives* (Washington, D.C.: GPO, 1999), 284.

25 Staff of the Senate Committee on the Budget, "President Clinton's 2000 Budget, A Brief Overview," February 1, 1999, p. 14.

26 The OMB FY 2000–2009 10-year budget projection assumed congressional enactment of the administration's proposals for Social Security reform.

27 This figure includes some RDT&E and procurement costs and, therefore, overstates the O&M budget shortfall. It was not possible to disaggregate these costs.

28 Henry H. Shelton, "Statement by General Henry H. Shelton, Chairman of the Joint Chiefs of Staff, to the Senate Armed Services Committee," January 5, 1999, p. 2 [emphasis in original].

29 Office of the Secretary of Defense, *FY 2000/2001 Biennial Budget Estimate, Operation and Maintenance Overview* (Washington, D.C.: U.S. Department of Defense, February 1999), 121.

30 Ibid., 155.

31 *FY 2000/2001 Biennial Budget Estimates, Operation and Maintenance, Army Data Book,* vol. 2 (Washington, D.C.: Department of Army, 1999), 117.

CHAPTER TWO
───────────────

DEFENSE LEGACIES OF THE 1990s

THE BELIEFS, PERCEPTIONS, AND DECISIONS OF THE 43RD PRESIDENT
AND 107TH CONGRESS WILL BE SHAPED AND INFLUENCED IN PART BY
THE MAJOR LEGACIES OF THE 1990s—largely created by the policies and
actions undertaken during the two terms of the Clinton presidency. It is
important to recall that the Clinton administration began its first term
in office with three strongly held beliefs about the future of the U.S.
military establishment.

First, the base force plan,[1] approved in 1991 by the Bush administration and implemented at that time by the military services, was too
large and composed of the wrong kinds of military capabilities for the
threats that the United States likely would face in the future. Second, the
base force plan was too expensive to maintain and operate given the new
president's domestic agenda and priorities—especially in a fiscal environment of rising federal deficits. Third and most important, President
Clinton and his first defense secretary, Les Aspin, held strong personal
convictions that it was possible for the United States to remain a global
power at substantially lower defense spending levels.[2]

The actions and decisions of the Clinton administration after seven
years in office reveal some surprising results. First, instead of large reductions and changes, the Clinton administration in fact made small reductions in the size of U.S. military forces and small changes in its
composition as the administration became reluctant to reduce military
forces, given its ambitious foreign policy agenda. The 1991 base force,
the 1993 BUR force,[3] and the 1997 QDR force[4] are more similar than

23

dissimilar in terms of size, composition, and character. Expansion—not elimination—of military missions took place as defense planning efforts shifted to consideration of and, later, incorporation of military missions in support of operations other than war (OOTW), multinational peace-keeping operations under United Nations auspices, and smaller-scale contingency operations. The number and types of missions that U.S. military forces must now be prepared to undertake and execute grew. Few military missions were eliminated as many capabilities still are desired and consequently retained even with smaller equipment inventories.

Second, as a result of the falling inflation rates and improving conditions in the U.S. economy, the Clinton administration was able—by using the inflation dividend from the defense budget—to reduce the federal deficit and to fund its domestic program initiatives and priorities. At the same time, the Clinton administration also was able to avoid making deep cuts in the defense budget because of improvements in DOD purchasing power. That is, DOD could offset potential budget cuts in nominal dollars and continue to pay for its current programs on a real-dollar basis because prices fell enough. This improved financial situation unfortunately was not large enough to pay for force modernization, given the actual costs during the previous five years of maintaining military readiness and conducting military operations and the large and growing costs of the peacetime U.S. defense establishment—despite repeated attempts by the Clinton administration to streamline it and reduce its costs.

Third, the Clinton administration continued to state and to insist that the United States can remain a global power at the substantially lower defense budgets it has submitted to Congress. The 1997 QDR projected that annual defense budgets of $266 billion during FY 1997–2015 would suffice. Such an amount was approximately $36 billion lower than the average budget levels proposed in January 1993 by the Bush administration in its last six-year defense plan. It also was approximately $143 billion lower than what was actually spent in FY 1985—the most recent peak year of military spending and a year in which the United States was acquiring those superpower military capabilities it still enjoys today. For five years until August–September 1998, senior U.S. defense officials strongly rejected and denied any suggestion that their defense plans were underfunded or not affordable.[5]

Only when advised by the Joint Chiefs of Staff, which finally warned in September 1998 that U.S. military forces were "showing increasing signs of serious wear" and DOD was facing annual budget shortfalls related to material readiness of at least $17.5 billion on a nominal-dollar basis beginning in FY 2000, did President Clinton agree eventually to a $112 billion defense budget increase for FY 2000–2005. While accepting the need for higher defense budgets, President Clinton set as a precondition for the increased defense spending the requirement that Congress in turn accept his proposals for Social Security reform and for spending the growing budget surplus projected for FY 2000–2009. If Congress were to refuse, Clinton indicated he would have no choice but to continue to reduce defense spending in order to comply with the provisions of the Balanced Budget Act of 1997.

As the 1990s draw to a close, in the national defense establishment six dominant conditions—legacies of the 1990s and the Clinton administration—will likely define, shape, and influence the beliefs, perceptions, and decisions of the 43rd president and 107th Congress on defense matters. At the end of the 1990s, the United States is faced with

- a world that is a dangerous place for U.S. national security interests, given the complexity, nature, and uncertainty of future threats;
- a military force that is overworked and tired because of the large number and diverse nature of contingency operations it has conducted in the 1990s—throughout the world and often for extended periods of time;
- a military force that is old and aging in terms of its military equipment and badly in need of modernization and replacement funds;
- a military and civilian leadership that is reluctant to make further force structure and personnel cuts, given present foreign policy objectives, diplomatic initiatives, and ongoing military operations;
- a defense infrastructure base that has significant excess capacity; and
- a defense budget that is greatly underpriced because of excessive optimism about future defense inflation.

Each of the six defense legacy conditions of the 1990s is briefly discussed in the following sections.

THE WORLD IS A DANGEROUS PLACE

There was in the 1990s much continuity, widespread agreement, and consensus about the nature of future threats to U.S. national security interests. The consensus is that the world will remain a complex, dynamic, dangerous, and uncertain place for the United States in the foreseeable future. Senior defense officials in both the Bush and Clinton administrations have held this view.

The end of the Cold War eliminated the threat of global war centered in Europe. This threat later was replaced by the threat of regional conflict posed by an aspiring regional hegemon, as demonstrated by Iraq in the Middle East during the 1990s. Secretary of Defense Dick Cheney wrote in his final *Annual Report to the President and the Congress,* published in January 1993:

> The focus of the new strategy is on meeting the regional threats and challenges that the United States is more likely to face in the future and on shaping the international security environment in ways that help to preclude the rise of hostile, nondemocratic powers aspiring to regional hegemony.[6]

The danger of regional conflicts was a major focus area of the assessment efforts conducted in both the 1993 BUR and 1997 QDR. The 1993 BUR concluded that the United States must be able to fight and win two major regional conflicts nearly simultaneously, and the 1997 QDR concluded that the United States must be able to defeat the initial enemy advance in two distant theaters in close succession. Today the danger of regional conflicts continues to dominate defense strategy, policy, and force planning efforts. In his *Annual Report to the President and the Congress,* published in February 1998, Secretary of Defense William S. Cohen wrote:

> The foremost regional danger to U.S. security is the continuing threat that hostile states with significant military power pose to al-

lies and friends in key regions. Between now and 2015, it is reasonable to assume that more than one such aspiring regional power will have both the motivation and the means to challenge U.S. interests militarily.[7]

U.S. defense policymakers and military planners also worried during the 1990s about other future threats. Many of these future threats were different and of a broader nature than the traditional security threats of the Cold War. At the end of the Bush administration, two other major threat issues dominated defense planning efforts:

- Crises stemming from instability in the developing world, and
- Dangers inherent in proliferation of weapons of mass destruction.[8]

These threats were replaced by a new set of threat priorities when the Clinton administration entered office in 1993. In addition to regional threats, Secretary of Defense Les Aspin warned of three other "dangers" facing the United States that demanded an immediate response:

- Nuclear dangers posed by nuclear weapons and other weapons of mass destruction located in the former Soviet Union or acquired by a rogue state or terrorist organization;
- Dangers to market and democratic reforms in the former Soviet Union, Eastern Europe, and elsewhere that could lead to turmoil; and
- Economic dangers to national security that could result if the United States failed to restore a strong, competitive, and growing economy and a restructured defense industrial base.[9]

Concerns about threats to democratic and market reforms and the economy faded in 1994 as the global economy expanded. These concerns were replaced by concerns of transnational problems of terrorism, the illegal drug trade, and international organized crime. By 1997, additional new concerns arose about information warfare and asymmetrical means of attacking U.S. forces and interests overseas and Americans at home. In 1999, a new concern emerged: threats to the U.S. homeland.

The 1999 *Annual Report to the President and Congress* describes accurately the threats to U.S. security interests that are diverse and span the entire threat spectrum:

- Large-scale, cross-border aggression in regions, such as Iraq, Iran, and North Korea, that are critical to U.S. interests;
- Flow of potentially dangerous technologies such as nuclear, biological, and chemical (NBC) weapons and their delivery systems; information warfare capabilities; or capabilities to provide or deny access to space throughout the world that could change the character of military challenges to U.S interests;
- Transnational dangers such as terrorism, illegal drug trade, international organized crime, environmental disasters, uncontrolled migrant flows, and other human emergencies that can destabilize regions of the world;
- Threats to the U.S. homeland such as those posed by ballistic missiles, NBC weapons, and information warfare;
- Failed states such as Yugoslavia and Zaire that can create internal conflicts and humanitarian crises and destabilize regions of the world; and
- Adversary use of asymmetric means—terrorism, NBC threats, information warfare, or environmental sabotage—to threaten or attack U.S. forces and interests overseas and at home.[10]

DOD must therefore plan and prepare for a broad range of plausible missions in an environment in which events are more complex and less predictable than they were in the past.

U.S. FORCES ARE OVERWORKED AND TIRED

A distinguishing characteristic of the 1990s was the large number of military operations conducted by U.S. military forces that involved small-scale conflicts and humanitarian and other similar contingencies—collectively referred to in DOD as smaller-scale contingency operations. During the entire Cold War period, U.S. military forces conducted a total of 16 smaller-scale contingency operations. In contrast, U.S. military forces conducted 45 smaller-scale contingency operations during FY 1990–1997: 16 initiated by President Bush and 29 initiated by President Clinton.[11] The latter represented a rate of one new deployment every nine weeks. In addition to the increase in both the frequency and total number of such operations in the Clinton administration, deployments also became extended—lasting several years. These deployments varied in terms of mission, size, forces, and the amount and nature of involvement or cooperation of U.S. allies and friends.

During FY 1993–1997, U.S. military forces

- enforced simultaneous naval embargoes in Bosnia, Iraq, and Haiti;
- enforced no-fly zones over Bosnia and northern and southern Iraq;
- carried out a show of force in the Taiwan Strait with two aircraft carrier battle groups;
- organized and provided the core of highly capable multinational forces in Haiti and Bosnia;
- conducted noncombatant evacuation operations or humanitarian operations in Liberia, Sierra Leone, Zaire, the Central African Republic, Cambodia, and Rwanda; and
- maintained an essential carrier presence in the Mediterranean Sea, Persian Gulf, and Indian Ocean.

In FY 1997, the United States was engaged in a total of 20 major military overseas operations. General Shelton, chairman of the Joint Chiefs of Staff, testified in 1998 that, on average, 43,000 service members were deployed each month in military operations overseas in FY 1997.[12] At the end of FY 1998, 218,957 (16 percent) of the total DOD active component force were stationed ashore overseas and another 139,564 (10 percent) of the total DOD active component were afloat—and likely forward deployed.[13] Senator McCain has cited congressional testimony by the chief of naval operations, Adm. Jay L. Johnson, that 50 percent of the navy's surface combatants were deployed around the globe in 1997 compared with 37 percent in 1992.[14]

The unexpected and uncertain nature of smaller-scale contingency operations placed enormous stress on the military services' operating tempo (OPTEMPO), personnel tempo, and deployment tempo in the 1990s. This stress was further aggravated by the military drawdown and defense budget decline. In short, the military services were doing more with fewer people and resources.

The impact of smaller-scale contingency operations varied by military service. Such operations reportedly had less of an impact on the navy and marines because of the degree to which these services were already forward deployed and the traditions of the two military services. However, in a written response to Senator John McCain's July 1998 letter inquiring about the current state of military readiness, Army Chief of Staff Gen. Dennis J. Reimer wrote:

> In the past nine years the Total Army has participated in 29 major deployments. In FY 1990 (Operation Desert Storm) we had an average of 154,324 soldiers deployed on any given day. In FY 1995, the average was 24,595 soldiers. In FY 1997, the average increased to 31,221 soldiers, and for FY 1998 it is about 29,000 soldiers. Compared with our end strength, these numbers may not seem significant. However, for every soldier deployed, two others are either preparing to go or recovering from a deployment.[15]

In a separate response to Senator McCain's letter, Air Force Chief of Staff Gen. Michael E. Ryan offered this reply:

> Anecdotal evidence suggests that the increased frequency of short notice/no notice deployment has had a very negative impact on the morale of our people. Airmen and units lose training to contingencies and must attempt to make up the lost training at the expense of recovery time and quality of life. Since 1991, contingency deployments have increased to four times that of the pre-war levels and have contributed to reduced retention rates which affect readiness.[16]

The impact of high OPTEMPO rates on individual units also varied widely. It was especially hard on so-called low-density, high-demand (LD/HD) assets such as U-2 RIVET Joint, E-3 AWACS, E-8 JSTARS, EA-6B, tactical UAVs, aerial refueling aircraft, and special operations forces—that are few in number but possess capabilities in high demand.

When engaged in a smaller-scale contingency operation, U.S. military forces must adopt and exercise a different set of attitudes, conduct, skills, and rules of engagement because these operations are not fight-and-win operations designed to inflict maximum damage on the enemy but, instead, are time-sensitive, damage-limited operations of restraint designed to promote and achieve very specific political, diplomatic, economic, or humanitarian objectives. U.S. military units consequently require additional time and resources to train for smaller-scale contingency operations and, later, to retrain for fight-and-win military operations. It was recently reported that 6 months of retraining, as a rule, are needed for smaller-scale contingency operations that last 6–12 months.[17]

The GAO in a recent field study observed the impact of OOTW on the services:

> OOTW has affected Army and Air Force units more than it has Navy and Marine Corps units. Returning units to their wartime mission capability levels during peacetime can take from several weeks for some support units to more than a year for some combat units, although in wartime the recovery period can be compressed if necessary. On the other hand, many units and/or personnel in the Army and the Air Force have been relatively unaffected by OOTW.[18]

U.S. FORCES ARE OLD AND AGING

Extensive and significant aging of the force took place in the 1990s and is expected to continue well into the twenty-first century. The breadth and depth of this force aging is unprecedented and will require a decade or more to reverse.

The air force, for example, reported that the average age of all its aircraft (active component and reserve component) will be 20 years in FY 2000, up from 13 years at the end of FY 1990. The average age will rise to 28 years in FY 2010 and, later, to 30 years in FY 2020.[19] The projected average age during this entire period is well above the steady state composite average age of 15 years for the QDR air force.

The air force reported that 38 percent of its combined active, guard, and reserve aircraft were 24 years old or older at the end of FY 1998. This gray share was up from 30 percent in FY 1990. This increase occurred even after a 30 percent reduction in aircraft inventory levels, from 8,959 aircraft in FY 1990 to 6,228 aircraft in FY 1998.[20]

In terms of individual components, the air force reported that aircraft with an age of 24 years or more accounted in FY 1998 for

- 41 percent of the air force active-duty aircraft;

- 47 percent of the air force reserve aircraft; and
- 25 percent of the Air National Guard aircraft.[21]

The navy will be composed of 314 ships and submarines in FY 2000. These ships and submarines will have an average age of 15 years. Ten years earlier, the average age was 16 years and the fleet was 53 percent larger, consisting of 482 ships and submarines. It is estimated the fleet average age will be 18 years by FY 2010—just below the steady state average age of 19 years. This small increase is attributed to low annual shipbuilding rates planned for FY 1997–2003.[22]

The breadth and depth of the DOD force aging problem is presented in table 2.1 in terms of 10 major DOD combat weapon classes. From FY 1990 to FY 2002, the expected change in average age is as follows:

- Four weapon classes will experience large increases (five or more years): strategic bombers, Apache helicopters, Abrams main battle tank, and Bradley fighting vehicles. The increases reflect the effects of the procurement holiday in the 1990s, during which annual production was simply halted;
- Four weapon classes will experience modest increases (two to five years): strategic airlift; air force attack/fighter aircraft; navy/marine corps attack/fighter aircraft; and navy surface combatants. The modest increases reflect decisions to continue some production (e.g., C-17, F-16, F/A-18, DDG-51) and at the same time retire a larger number of older aircraft (e.g., C-141, F-4, F-111, A-6) and ships (e.g., CG-16, CG-26, DDG-2, DDG-37); and
- Two weapon classes will experience a slight increase (two or fewer years) or no increase: navy attack submarines and amphibious ships. This reflects the fact that purchases kept up with retirements of the smaller force during this period.

Table 2.1 also shows, in terms of the 10 major DOD combat weapon classes, that

- six classes will be near or well in excess of their estimated service half-life in FY 2002; this will increase by three by FY 2010; and
- six classes will have an average age in FY 2010 that is at least four years older than in FY 2002.

Table 2.1
Force Aging Trends

Weapon Class	Half-Life (years)	Average Age (measured in years)			Out-Year Plans (quantities, est.)
		FY 1990	FY 2002	FY 2010	
Strategic Bombers	15–25	22	28	36	No purchases
Strategic Airlift	20	21	25	23	50 C-17
Attack/Fighter Aircraft					
Air Force	11–15	12	16	20	Approx. 500 F-22 and JSF
Navy/Marine Corps	10–15	10	13	14	Approx. 680 F/A-18 and JSF
Attack Submarines	12–15	14	14	17	2 SSN-774
Surface Combatants	17–20	12	14	19	12 DDG-51
Amphibious Ships	20	19	20	15	10 LPD-17
Apache Helicopters	15	3	13	21	No purchases
Abrams Main Battle Tanks	20	4	15	23	No purchases
Bradley Fighting Vehicles	20	4	14	22	No purchases

Source: MSTI estimates based on data from DOD.

Finally, the projected FY 2010 average ages as shown in table 2.1 are based on full funding of the services' procurement plans. In the event these procurement quantities are not funded, the average age will grow higher unless inventories are reduced again.

The decisions of the 1997 QDR did very little to change the average age estimates projected for FY 2002. The decisions instead assured additional increases in the average age of aircraft, ships and submarines, and tracked combat vehicles for most of the next decade: the 1997 QDR made no significant changes in equipment inventories; provided for no increases in spending on major DOD procurement programs; reduced the total production and maximum production rates for F-22, joint strike fighter (JSF), and F/A-18 E/F aircraft; and provided for a less than steady state shipbuilding rate for surface combatant ships.

Efforts to halt, reverse, and overcome force aging are in part determined and influenced by the actual age distribution of equipment. Actual age distribution reflects the long-term effects of past procurement decisions and actual production or delivery rate experience. For many DOD weapon classes today, the force aging problem reflects the interaction between the high annual production rates of the late 1970s and 1980s and the low production rates or no procurements of the 1990s—in the context of a significantly smaller force structure and equipment inventory levels.

Because 20 to 25 years have passed since the start of the most recent defense procurement modernization cycle, the smaller QDR force is starting to reach the end of its useful life—almost all at once. As this occurs, senior defense officials will be gradually compelled to decide on force replacement and modernization programs primarily on the bases of delivery time and the relative maximum benefit to be derived from the use of scarce procurement dollars. Near-term operational considerations will take precedence over long-term considerations. Without procurement dollars to purchase replacements, senior defense officials will have no choice but to accept reductions in QDR force capabilities at the moment the end of useful life is reached. In response to this situation, defense planners will turn increasingly toward technology to offset losses in military capabilities. They will find, however, technology advances alone will not offset the large potential reductions in force size and maintain acceptable risk levels.

The implications of equipment aging are not easy to quantify, but they are expected to be significant. Two senior air force acquisition and logistics officers testified before the Subcommittee on Military Procurement of the House Armed Services Committee in February 1999:

> While it is difficult to quantify the exact impact aging has on Air Force readiness, we are confident it has significantly contributed to the declining MC (mission-capability) rates and increasing Operations and Support costs. This alone is cause for concern over implications of maintaining fleets for longer and longer periods of time.[23]

Moreover, a recent study[24] conducted by the RAND Project Air Force concluded:

If recent [cost] trends continued, annual costs for those two activities [aircraft programmed depot maintenance (PDM) and engine support] would initially rise at a modest rate [from 1998 to 2010]. Then, in the second decade of the next century, they would *accelerate*, mainly because of the increasing age of the cargo and tanker fleets.[25]

As a result of these trends, RAND Project Air Force analysts estimated that the annual air force PDM and engine support would more than double, from $2 billion in FY 1998 to $5–6 billion in 2020.

The extended use of military equipment often results in one or more of the following:

- Lower equipment availability rates as more and more time needs to be spent on inspections and repairs, as well as the unpredictable nature and extent of unplanned maintenance and repair problems;
- Higher incidence of equipment failure or accidents that may or may not involve injury or loss of human life;
- Less flexibility on the part of military operations planners and acquisition planners in reacting and responding to unforeseen maintenance and repair problems;
- Higher maintenance and repair workloads and costs for acquiring and installing replacement parts because the number of qualified suppliers and maintainers has dwindled and their special skills must be used inefficiently.

In addition, O&M savings expected from the introduction of new weapon systems are often more than counterbalanced by the higher maintenance and repair costs related to keeping older equipment longer in the force. In 1998 the commandant of the Marine Corps, Gen. Charles C. Krulak, testified before the Senate Committee on Armed Services:

Each successive year this equipment, much of which has exceeded its projected service life, breaks down more often, and must spend more time awaiting and undergoing repair. It is lost to the unit for training. The associated maintenance costs continue to rise, leading to increasing investments in O&M. To comply with the Department of Defense guidance and our congressionally mandated role, we must take money from our procurement, research and development, military construction and quality of life accounts to fund these near-term readiness requirements. In many cases we have passed the point where this equipment has consumed more dollars in spare assemblies, time, manpower, and service life extension programs (SLEPs) than would be spent in procuring new equipment. Even within our O&M accounts themselves, money which would normally be dedicated to training and training support functions is currently being spent to maintain this aging equipment. It is a vicious cycle, and one that becomes increasingly expensive to stop with time. As the commercial says, "You can pay me now, or you can pay me later!"[26]

The extensive and substantial aging of U.S. military forces also must be viewed in the context of the profound changes under way in DOD maintenance organizations and supporting industrial base as a result of smaller defense budgets, manpower reductions, new maintenance policies, and defense management initiatives—most notably defense acquisition reforms. The National Research Council (NRC) Committee on Aging of U.S. Air Force Aircraft, for example, found that, although the air force has been very successful during the past 20 years in maintaining aircraft structural safety, serious concerns arise about aircraft structural safety in the future:

> [T]he extended use of old aircraft, coupled with the potentially adverse effects of reduced military budgets; reduced manpower; grade structure limitations; increased reliance on contractor maintenance; the elimination or relaxation of military regulations, standards, and specifications; and possible complacency of air force management, may make this past success rather fragile. The committee believes it will take aggressive air force management and engineering actions to counter this deterioration in capability and loss in ASIP [Aircraft Structural Integrity Program] oversight and to prevent further deterioration in the future.[27]

The NRC concerns are equally applicable to the aviation forces of the army, the marine corps, and the navy as well as to other DOD force elements—ships, submarines, and tracked combat vehicles. Thus aging military equipment coupled with diminished capabilities of the defense maintenance organizations and industrial base raise additional new concerns about equipment safety, performance, availability, and reliability —all in the context of contribution to overall mission success.

It is not possible today to know how the aging of U.S. military forces will influence and shape perceptions and actions of senior U.S. national security civilian and military officials in the future.[28] It is likely that equipment aging will first be seen in terms of loss of equipment availability and, therefore, manifest itself as a U.S. force readiness problem. This in turn may require military contingency planners to develop alternative concepts of military operations with the use of different equipment as well as to alter or modify existing U.S. military contingency plans. It is also possible that a military operation will fail in the future because of equipment failure. As equipment-aging-related readiness problems emerge, the willingness to use military force may decline because political and military leaders will grow more reluctant to recommend it or feel less confident that military objectives can be successfully attained.

THERE IS GREAT RELUCTANCE TO CUT FORCE STRUCTURE AND PERSONNEL

1993 BUR — Force Structure Results

The Clinton administration entered office with the strong belief that the base force plan was too large and composed of the wrong kinds of military capabilities for the threats the United States would likely face in the future. Instead of large reductions and changes, however, the Clinton administration in fact made only small reductions in the size of U.S. military forces and small changes in its composition—except for naval forces. The 1991 base force, 1993 BUR force, and 1997 QDR force are more similar than dissimilar in terms of size, composition, and character.

In his first major national security speech, presidential candidate Bill Clinton stated ". . . we need to replace our Cold War military structure with a smaller, more flexible mix of capabilities" that retains a survivable nuclear deterrent force, emphasizes rapid deployment of forces, maintains the U.S. technological lead, and is supported by better intelligence.[29] He also urged that the United States lead international efforts to establish a United Nations rapid deployment force that could be "used for purposes beyond traditional peacekeeping, such as standing guard at the borders of countries threatened by aggression; preventing attacks on civilians; providing humanitarian relief; and combating terrorism and drug trafficking."[30]

President Clinton's first secretary of defense, Les Aspin, also was a leading opponent of the base force plan, especially in his capacity as the chairman of the House Committee on Armed Services. In early 1992 Aspin, then in the House of Representatives, published three major defense policy papers highly critical of the base force plan and proposed four "illustrative" DOD force structure alternatives at substantially lower defense budget levels.[31] According to Aspin, the base force plan "did not represent a new conceptual approach for a new security era but essentially 'less of the same,' that is, a downsized force largely shaped by Cold War priorities."[32] The base force was "still a robust force that hedged strongly against the risk that the Soviet threat might be revived."[33]

Aspin instead argued and advocated throughout 1992 that, when policymakers decide on the future size and shape of U.S. military forces, "it is critical *to identify threats to U.S. interests that are sufficiently important that Americans would consider the use of force to secure them.*"[34] DOD force planning therefore must be threat based, he contended.

In his third paper, Aspin wrote that threat-based force planning was essential for two reasons.

> First, no other approach to force planning tells you how much is enough. Top-down force planning—what is being practiced in the Pentagon as they take successive cuts out of the budget—will leave us with a smaller version of the force built for the Cold War. If the force is not built from the bottom up on a clear threat assessment, then there is no way of knowing whether it is the right size or kind for the new era.
>
> Second, what citizens look for from their national security establishment is protection of their vital interests against things they

perceive as threatening to them. In this era of belt tightening, our citizens understandably may be reluctant to pay for defense unless there is a clear linkage between the forces and the threats those forces are designed to deal with.[35]

As President Clinton and Secretary of Defense Aspin entered office, right-sizing of U.S. forces replaced downsizing as the mantra for senior DOD civilian and military leadership. This was most evident during the 1993 BUR: "We undertook the Bottom-Up Review to select the right strategy, force structure, and modernization programs, and supporting industrial base and infrastructure to provide for America's defense in the post–Cold War era."[36]

In addition, President Clinton and Secretary of Defense Aspin strongly believed the right-sized U.S. force would be smaller and less costly than the base force. This conviction is clearly visible in the president's economic plan in 1993. Even before the March 1993 start of the BUR—on February 17, 1993—President Clinton presented to a joint session of Congress an economic plan that proposed cutting defense outlays by $112 billion on a nominal basis during FY 1994–1998.[37] The economic plan also described the new administration's approach to national security:

> Reducing the size of the military to provide for other needs, therefore, is not our purpose. Rather, our goal is to reshape our forces to provide us with the capabilities we need to defend our continuing interests, deal with new problems and threats, and contribute to the promotion of democracy, prosperity, and security in a new world. . . .
>
> Our defense strategy will be driven by a fresh assessment of the challenges that require the use of American military force. . . .
>
> These forces will be consistent with the design we have promised: 1.4 million men and women on active duty, a strong, integrated reserve and a capable forward presence of roughly 100,000 troops in Europe. Our military will be *mobile* (with the sealift and airlift it requires), *agile* (with new technologies and integrated doctrine which allows it to dominate by maneuver, speed and technological superiority), *precise* (to reduce the loss of life in combat), *flexible*

(to operate with diverse partners in diverse regions), *smart* (with the intelligence and communications it needs for the diverse threats it will face) and, especially *ready* (given the unpredictability of new threats). . . .

As we undertake a major strategic review over the coming months, we will identify new changes, savings and additions that will fit our new strategy.[38]

Thus, before the threat-based force assessment was begun, the president's economic plan had already established the budget, personnel levels, and modernization priorities (mobile, agile, precise, flexible, smart, and ready) for the BUR. Senior DOD officials insisted, however, that their deliberations during the BUR were not constrained. They suggested it was merely coincidental that the BUR arrived at a set of decisions that matched the guidance of the president's economic plan.

The 1993 BUR was described by the White House and senior defense officials as the first comprehensive assessment of U.S. defense needs in the post-Soviet era. It also was characterized as involving close collaboration between the civilian staff of the Office of the Secretary of Defense and the military professionals in the Joint Staff, the service staffs, and the headquarters staffs of the Unified Combatant Commands.

Table 2.2 presents the force levels in FY 1990 and the goals established for the 1991 base force, 1993 BUR force, and 1997 QDR force. Table 2.2 shows that during the 1993 BUR and the 1997 QDR the Clinton administration did not make many force structure changes to the base force plan it inherited from the Bush administration even though Clinton imposed large budget cuts. Few changes occurred despite the emphasis on threat-based force planning, right-sizing the force, and close collaboration between civilian and military officials throughout all levels of the DOD establishment.

Table 2.2 shows that the 1993 BUR reduced the force structure of the 1991 base force plan as follows:

- 2 army active divisions (1 armored/1 mechanized), from 12 to 10;
- 2 air force active tactical fighter wing–equivalents (FWEs), from 15 to 13;
- 1 navy aircraft carrier, from 12 to 11;

Table 2.2
Changes in Force Structure

Major Forces	Bush Administration			Clinton Administration		
	FY 1990	1991 Base Force	Change[a]	1993 BUR Force	1997 QDR Force	Change[b]
Army						
Divisions (AC)	18	12	-6	10	10	-2
Brigades (RC)	57	34	-23	42	42[c]	+8
Marine Expeditionary Force (AC/RC)	3/1	3/1	NC/NC	3/1	3/1	NC/NC
Navy						
Aircraft Carriers (AC/RC)	15/1	12/1	-3/NC	11/1	12/0	+1/-1
Carrier Air Wings (AC/RC)	13/2	11/2	-2/NC	10/1	10/1	-1/-1
Surface Combatants (AC/RC)	203/0	141/0	-62/NC	116/10	106/10	-35/+10
Amphibious Readiness Group (AC)	12	11	-1	12	12	+1
Battle Force Ships (AC)	546	430	-116	346	298	-132
Air Force						
Strategic Bombers (AC)	268	176	-92	114	187	+11
Fighter Wing-Equivalents (AC/RC)	24/12	15/11	-9/-1	13/11	12/8	-3/-3

Sources: Cheney, *Annual Report to the President and the Congress,* 1992, 27; Aspin, *Annual Report to the President and the Congress,* 1994, 1994, 27; and Cohen, *Annual Report to the President and the Congress,* 1998, 27.

a   Change from FY 1990 to 1991 Base Force

b   Change from 1991 Base Force to 1997 QDR Force.

c   Although the 1997 QDR recommended a "smaller" army reserve component, the number of army reserve brigades has remained unchanged.

- 1 navy carrier air wing, from 11 to 10;
- 84 navy ships and submarines, from 430 to 346.

The 1993 BUR also established 15 enhanced separate readiness Army National Guard combat brigades that are to be capable of reinforcing army combat forces in regional contingencies within 90 days of their mobilization. This change resulted in a net increase of eight army reserve brigades.

The relatively small changes to U.S. force structure generally disappointed the Congress, the press, and the public. In his first press conference disclosing the results of the BUR, Secretary Aspin offered the following reply to a reporter's skeptical question of "what's really new?"

> If you look at the lay-out of what we're trying to do here, we've got some initiatives in this bill that you would not have had before. You're dealing explicitly with two MRCs (Major Regional Contingencies), and you've got identified the possible bad guys that you may need to deal with in the MRCs. What you've got is, of course, a force structure which is smaller than what we had before, but we got a force structure which in some cases has got more, . . . it is a defense budget which has changed its focus from one threat— Soviet Union/Warsaw Pact—to a new world of a whole new bunch of threats. That shapes the budget. That is what shapes it. That is what's new. It's new in its fundamental propositions. We then go through and see what we've got to work with. We're going to need some forces, as we will see, in terms of R&D. We're going to need some capabilities that we don't now have. This drives you to consideration that there are certain kinds of capabilities that we don't have in our inventory. *But what we've got in the first instance is a set of weapon systems and force structure that are designed for a different purpose.*[39]

1997 QDR — Force Structure Results

The second strategic review of the Clinton administration, the 1997 QDR, also made few changes to U.S. military force structure even though Congress and others outside the DOD expressed concerns and

Table 2.3
QDR Force Structure Alternatives — Three Paths

Major Forces	Near-Term Focus Path 1	Long-Term Focus Path 2	Balanced Focus Path 3*
Army			
Divisions (AC)	10	8	10
Brigades (RC)	42	33	Smaller
Marine Expeditionary Force	3	Smaller	3
Navy			
Aircraft Carriers (AC/RC)	12	10	12
Surface Combatants (AC/RC)	131	108	116
Air Force			
Fighter Wing-Equivalents (AC/RC)	13/7	10/6	12/8

Source: Cohen, *Report of the Quadrennial Defense Review,* 21–22.
* Path 3 was selected by the QDR.

reservations about the long-term affordability of the BUR force. The 1997 QDR eliminated 4 air force tactical FWEs (13/11 compared with 12/8) and 48 additional navy ships and submarines (346 compared with 298); see table 2.2. It also revalidated and reaffirmed the need for 12 air-craft carrier battle groups and 12 amphibious readiness groups to meet overseas presence requirements and the need for 10 active army divisions and 20 air force tactical FWEs to execute two nearly simultaneous major-theater wars with moderate risk.

In the *Report of the Quadrennial Defense Review,* Secretary of Defense Cohen described the 1997 QDR force structure reductions as "modest" and "offset in part by enhanced capabilities of new systems and a streamlined support structure."[40] He also emphasized that the QDR force "retains sufficient force structure to sustain global American leadership and meet the full range of today's requirements" and is "fiscally executable."[41]

The reluctance of the Clinton administration to consider larger cuts in military force structure is also demonstrated by the three force

Strategic Objectives of Alternative QDR Force Postures[1]

Path 1
Focus on Near-Term Demands

Defense resources are allocated on the basis of securing "international stability in the near term through global presence and deterrence of regional aggression, while largely deferring preparations for the possibility of more demanding security challenges in the future."

Path 2
Preparing for a More Distant Future

Defense resources are allocated on the basis of ensuring "the long-term dominance of U.S. forces by preparing now for the emergence of more challenging threats in the future while accepting reductions in our capabilities to meet near-term demands."

Path 3
Balance Current Demands and an Uncertain Future

Defense resources are allocated on the basis of sustaining "U.S. global leadership through this uncertain period by balancing capabilities to address near-term challenges with focused investments to counter longer-term threats."

Note

1 Cohen, *Report of the Quadrennial Defense Review,* 21–22.

structure alternatives considered by the 1997 QDR (referred to at the time as force structure paths); see table 2.3. (A description of the three alternative force structure paths is also provided.) From a budget and finance perspective, the three QDR force structure alternatives were variations of the same force. They do not represent a serious attempt to deal with or resolve the overall DOD strategy–resources mismatch described in chapter 1 of this book.

Events in Somali, Bosnia, Haiti, the Middle East, and the Korean Peninsula gradually forced the Clinton administration to accept the view that the current size of U.S. military forces is about the right size—

given the rapidly changing international security environment, the administration's vision the United States remain engaged abroad, and the current ambitious demands of its foreign policy and diplomatic initiatives. The administration's preoccupation with today's current operational needs is best demonstrated by the reasons offered in the *Report of the Quadrennial Defense Review* for rejecting QDR path 2, Preparing for a More Distant Future.

The strategic objective of path 2 is to ensure "the long-term dominance of U.S. forces by preparing now for the emergence of more challenging threats in the future while accepting reductions in our capabilities to meet near-term demands." Compared with the approved QDR force (see table 2.2 for QDR force strength), path 2 would cut two additional active army divisions, nine reserve army brigades, two active air force tactical FWEs, and eight additional surface combatants and would

- require reductions in permanently stationed forces, affecting the U.S. commitment to keep roughly 100,000 military personnel in Europe and Asia;
- reduce markedly the rotation commitments of naval, air, and ground forces;
- restrict U.S. flexibility to exercise and train with allies and friends or to increase temporarily overseas deployments;
- increase significantly the personnel tempo and deployment tempo for many units, potentially raising longer-term concerns about personnel retention;
- require the United States to be more selective in conducting smaller-scale contingency operations, particularly those that have the potential to last a long time;
- place greater reliance on early and extensive use of reserve component forces;
- anticipate significantly larger contributions from allies and friends; and
- rely on "swinging" both combat and support forces from one theater to another to defeat large-scale aggression in two regions.[42]

Given the current international security environment, the force structures of the 1991 base force, 1993 BUR force, and 1997 QDR force appear to represent a floor in terms of the relative size of the military force required by the United States to be a global power engaged in the world. The three strategic defense reviews also suggest that little has changed since 1991–1993 in terms of U.S. thinking about the overall size of U.S. military force structure and personnel levels in the post–Cold War era. This state of thinking will likely continue at least through 2001, which will be 12 years after the collapse of the Berlin Wall. Although the 1991 base force was sized to respond to the possible reemergence of a Soviet-led global threat, both the 1993 BUR and the 1997 QDR acknowledged that the United States still requires a force level and a personnel level similar in size to those during the Cold War although for a different purpose—to respond to two major theaters of war in close succession. The major problem, however, is that in 2001 the United States will not have adjusted its budgets to match its military strategy and programs. Equally important, the White House and DOD have yet to prepare the American public for the necessity of higher U.S. military spending.

Changes in Manpower Levels

Given its great reluctance to make large cuts in DOD force structure, it is not surprising to learn that the Clinton administration accordingly has made only modest reductions in DOD personnel levels. See table 2.4, which compares the combined manpower decisions made in the 1993 BUR and 1997 QDR with earlier decisions in the 1991 base force plan.

For the 10-year period FY 1994–2003, the combined 1993 BUR and 1997 QDR decisions are expected to reduce 1991 base force levels by

- 266,000 active-duty military personnel, 16 percent;
- 85,000 reserve military personnel, 9 percent; and
- 269,000 DOD civilian-worker full-time equivalents (FTEs), 30 percent.

Compared with private industry in the 1990s, DOD has adopted a generally passive, employee-friendly approach toward downsizing its workforce, relying largely on retirement, voluntary separation incentive pay (buyouts),[43] and voluntary early retirement[44] to reduce end-strength levels. Of the 219,000 DOD civilian worker positions eliminated from FY 1993 to FY 1998,

Table 2.4
End-Strength Levels (thousands)

Personnel	Bush Administration			Clinton Administration		
	FY 1990	1991 Base Force	Change[a]	1993 BUR Force	1997 QDR Force	Change[b]
Active Duty	2,070	1,626	-444	1,418	1,360	-266
Reserve	1,128	920	-208	893	835	-85
Civilian Full-Time Equivalents	1,073	909	-164	728	640	-269

Sources: Cheney, *Annual Report to the President and the Congress*, 1992, 27; Aspin, *Annual Report to the President and the Congress*, 1994, 27; and Cohen, *Annual Report to the President and the Congress*, 1998, 27.

[a] Change from FY 1990 to 1991 Base Force.

[b] Change from 1991 Base Force to 1997 QDR Force.

- 130,000 (59 percent) accepted buyouts,
- 54,000 (25 percent) accepted voluntary early retirement,
- 19,000 (9 percent) were involuntarily let go, and
- 16,000 (7 percent) retired or chose voluntarily to terminate their employment.[45]

Because the separation terms were generous, the overall budgetary effect of this approach was to incur higher payroll and employee benefit costs for a longer period.

DOD currently anticipates that most 1997 QDR personnel reductions will come from success achieved by outsourcing, reengineering, and streamlining DOD infrastructure activities and conducting additional rounds of base realignment and closure (BRAC). DOD expects to outsource 229,000 positions in the period from FY 1997 to FY 2005 and projects $11 billion (nominal dollars) in cumulative savings and $3.4 billion (nominal dollars) in annual recurring savings thereafter.[46] A total of 58,000 positions were competed in FY 1997 and FY 1998.[47]

Senior DOD officials continue to hope that, as work is outsourced, current DOD civilian workers will simply change employers—from government to private industry. Skill levels therefore will be maintained, and industry will be able to perform the work at substantially lower costs—in both the near term and the long term. This DOD view will be challenged by the labor realities of a smaller U.S. defense industry (with high wages for special skills) and globalization (with labor diverted to satisfy the higher-profit product lines of the global marketplace).

THERE IS AN EXCESS OF INFRASTRUCTURE

As U.S. military force structure and personnel levels fell in the 1990s, excess base capacity became an issue. DOD efforts to eliminate or reduce this excess base capacity proceeded slowly. Although a total of 97 major military bases will be closed by FY 2001, infrastructure reductions continued to lag behind reductions in force structure, personnel, and the overall defense budget. DOD estimated a total excess base capacity of 23 percent exists at 259 major military installations it examined in April 1998.[48] According to DOD, elimination of this excess base capacity would correspond to approximately 55 additional military bases, which coincidentally is the combined number of base closings recommended by the 1993 and 1995 BRAC commissions. The April 1998 report may also be underestimating excess base capacity if the formation of joint service installations is encouraged and pursued, as was recommended by the 1997 National Defense Panel (NDP).[49] The Clinton administration has proposed to Congress since 1997 that additional BRAC rounds be conducted. Congress has rejected the administration proposal each time.

On the basis of the success of the 1988 BRAC round,[50] Congress enacted the Defense Base Closure and Realignment Act of 1990, which authorized three additional BRAC rounds in 1991, 1993, and 1995. When reductions are completed in FY 2001, the four BRAC rounds will have reduced the number of major military domestic bases by 19 percent— from 493 bases in FY 1990 to 398 bases in FY 2002.[51] DOD currently projects these base closures will generate net savings on a nominal basis of $3.7 billion through FY 1999 and $25 billion through FY 2003 and will yield recurring annual savings of $5.6 billion every year thereafter.[52]

Infrastructure reductions, however, lagged relative to reductions made in force structure, personnel, and the overall defense budget during the 1990s. Figure 2.1 shows relative changes since FY 1990, including those currently projected and based on the February 1999 DOD military

Figure 2.1
Selected DOD Resource Indicators, FY 1990–2005

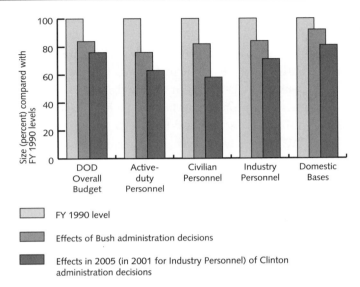

FY 1990 level

Effects of Bush administration decisions

Effects in 2005 (in 2001 for Industry Personnel) of Clinton administration decisions

Sources: MSTI, based on data reported in Office of the Under Secretary of Defense (Comptroller), *National Defense Budget Estimates for FY 2000* (Washington, D.C.: Department of Defense, March 1999), 77, 211; and *Base Closures and Realignment Report* (Washington, D.C.: Department of Defense, March 1995).

spending plan for FY 2000–2005. By FY 2005 the number of domestic military bases will be 81 percent of the number in FY 1990, reflecting the closure of 97 bases during the 1990s. The DOD budget will be 76 percent of its FY 1990 size. At the same time, active-duty personnel end strength and DOD civilian FTEs will decline to 64 percent and 58 percent, respectively. In FY 2001, defense industry employment is expected to be 71 percent of its FY 1990 levels.

Finally, if DOD was permitted to close 55 additional bases as it proposed in April 1998, DOD infrastructure by FY 2011 would decline to 70 percent of its FY 1990 size. Based on the relative reductions in personnel and budget, additional base closures are clearly warranted in numbers substantially greater than what was proposed by DOD in April 1998. To reach 60 percent of Cold War numbers, for example, new BRAC rounds would need to recommend a total of 100 additional bases for closure—slightly less than twice the current DOD proposal.

In FY 1997, the DOD infrastructure base occupied roughly 40,000 square miles of land, an area the size of Virginia. The physical plant is valued at $500 billion. In addition to mission and mission-support facilities, the DOD infrastructure base also provided housing for more than 293,000 families and 400,000 unmarried service members.[53]

On the basis of the recommendations of the 1997 QDR and the NDP, DOD submitted to Congress in 1998 and again in 1999 draft legislation for authorization of two additional BRAC rounds in 2001 and 2005, equal in size to BRAC '93 and BRAC '95. According to DOD, the additional BRAC rounds would save, on a recurring annual basis, $3.4 billion beginning in FY 2012.

In April 1998, as part of a congressionally mandated report on base realignment and closure, DOD reported among other things the results of its excess base capacity analysis. DOD found the magnitude of the excess base capacity varied by military department and by type of military installation that each military department operates:

- Army: 20–28 percent;
- Navy and Marine Corps: 21–22 percent;
- Air Force: 20–24 percent;
- Defense Logistics Agency: 35 percent.

Table 2.5 on pages 52 and 53 summarizes the 1998 DOD excess capacity estimates by military department and installation category.[54]

Although it claimed excess base capacity exists, the April 1998 report at the same time was ambiguous, vague, and cautious about the exact number of military bases that should be closed:

> The results indicate that the amount of excess capacity is sufficiently large to justify authorization of new BRAC rounds. The method's results, however, cannot predict the exact nature of potential closures or realignments in each category of installation because it does not compare base capacity with absolute requirements for that capacity. Nor, as noted previously, does it assess particular characteristics of specific bases, which are critical to any specific decision. For example, this analysis assigned each base to only one installation category. In fact, most bases support more than one

category. As a consequence, all categories of installations would be considered in subsequent BRAC rounds.[55]

The importance and significance of closing additional bases was underscored by Secretary of Defense Cohen in his forwarding message to the April 1998 report:

> To put the value of BRAC in perspective, two new rounds of base closure would yield about $20 billion in savings by 2015. What is the value of $20 billion? In the Air Force, $20 billion would buy 450 Joint Strike Fighter aircraft (two-thirds of the air force's total JSF procurement planned through 2015). In the Navy, $20 billion would buy both of the CVX next-generation aircraft carriers and 12 of the 32 new surface combatant planned for procurement by 2015. In the Army, $20 billion would cover the entire procurement in this period of two systems needed to create a digitized force: the Comanche helicopter and the Crusader artillery system. Finally, in the Marine Corps, $20 billion would provide for almost all of the Joint Strike Fighters planned for procurement during this period and all of the Advanced Amphibious Assault Vehicles.[56]

The current DOD rationale of the need for additional base closures, as stated first in the April 1998 report, is as follows:

> Without congressional authorization for more BRAC rounds, many defense reform efforts will fail to achieve their full potential, and DOD will miss opportunities to channel potential savings to higher priorities. . . . BRAC is an integral part of the Department's defense strategy. Congressional approval of new BRAC authorities will enhance DOD's ability to carry out the military strategy outlined in the QDR. *In the absence of future BRAC rounds, DOD could fail to fully support the operational concepts that are central to the Revolution in Military Affairs and fail to make the best of the opportunities created by the Revolution in Business Affairs.*[57]

In his same forwarding message, Secretary of Defense Cohen warned: "Without the certainty of the BRAC today, we will have to adjust our plans for modernization, force structure, and quality of life."[58]

Table 2.5
Excess Base Capacity, 1998

Military Services and Categories of Installations	Change in Capacity relative to Force Structure since 1989 (percentage of 2003 capacity)
Defense Logistics Agency	
Distribution Depots	38
Supply Centers	29
Total, Defense Logistics Agency	**35**
Army	
Maneuver	2–14
Major Training (AC)	22
Major Training (RC)	1
Depots	No increase
Administration	No increase–19
Industrial	38
Schools	38–39
Test and Evaluation, Laboratories	39–62
Total, Army	**20–28**
Navy	
Bases, Navy	34
Bases, Marine Corps	16–29
Air Stations	13
Ordnance Stations	16–26
Training	23–53
Training Air Stations	21
Supply Installations	44
Aviation Depots	No increase
Shipyards	6
Logistics Bases, Marine Corps	No increase
Test and Evaluation, and Laboratories	18
Construction Battalion Centers	No increase
Inventory Control Points, Navy	48
Administration	15
Total, Navy	**21–22**

(continued)

Table 2.5 (continued)
Excess Base Capacity, 1998

Military Services and Categories of Installations	Change in Capacity relative to Force Structure since 1989 (percentage of 2003 capacity)
Air Force	
Reserve Component	69
Air National Guard	No increase
Depots	No increase
Education and Training	No increase–28
Missiles and Large Aircraft	17–18
Small Aircraft	28–42
Space Operations	No increase
Product Centers, Laboratories, and Test and Evaluation	24–38
Administration	21
Total, Air Force	**20–24**

Source: William S. Cohen, *Report of the Department of Defense on Base Realignment and Closure* (Washington, D.C.: Department of Defense, April 1998), 16–17.

This rationale and the importance of additional base closures were emphasized again in the FY 2000 DOD budget submission and the annual report of the secretary of defense:

> Important decisions about future BRAC rounds need to be made in the near future since the Department's growing modernization program peaks in the period after FY 2005 and additional resources must be found to support it. Eliminating excess capacity in infrastructure early in the next decade could yield billions in savings necessary to finance modernization and readiness programs, and facilitate realization of the goals contained in *Joint Vision 2010*.[59]

Although the Congress did approve the base closures and realignments of the 1990s, it nevertheless still remains extremely reluctant to approve more. Besides the easily understood concerns about the economic and political impacts of base closing on states, communities, and constituents, congressional reluctance was driven largely by additional concerns:

- The integrity of the BRAC process following (1) President Clinton's actions in 1995 to privatize work in place and thereby save jobs at air logistic centers in Sacramento, California, and San Antonio, Texas, instead of close these centers as the 1995 BRAC had recommended and (2) White House actions in 1998 surrounding the award of a multimillion-dollar contract for maintenance work involving the air logistics center in Sacramento, California;
- The accuracy of actual cost savings and expenses incurred as a result of BRACs already approved;
- The loss of large, expensive-to-acquire facilities that could never be regained if a future threat required a defense buildup. "Do we think this is as big as DOD is ever going to get?" one congressional aide reportedly asked;[60] and
- The timing and size of future base-closure savings to offset budget shortfalls in military readiness, quality of life, and modernization programs. Many members of Congress believe savings from new BRAC rounds do little to offset near-term budget shortfalls; are too small to eliminate the entire budget shortfall; and again divert attention from the need for hard decisions about force structure, acquisition programs, and the current administration's role in underfunding defense.

Finally, in the context of a $280 billion annual defense budget, many members of Congress do not believe an estimated recurring annual savings of $3.6 billion is large enough to justify the political costs they must endure when they cast a vote for base closure, especially when their states or districts are involved.

THE DEFENSE BUDGET IS UNDERPRICED

Today's Strong Economy

As a result of falling inflation and improving conditions in the U.S. economy during the 1990s, the Clinton administration—by using the inflation dividend from the defense budget—was able to reduce the federal deficit and fund its domestic program initiatives and priorities. At

Table 2.6
Comparison of Bush and Clinton DOD Budgets, FY 1994–1999

Summaries of DOD Budgets	FY 2000 Dollars (billions)
Bush Administration Final DOD Budget Plan January 1993	1,782
Changed economic and budget assumptions	(112)
Internal DOD actions	(50)
Congressional actions, rescissions, and reprogramming	26
Supplementals[a]	26
Clinton Administration DOD Budget July 1999	1,672
Net Total Spending Change	(110)

Sources: MSTI, derived from data reported in Office of the Under Secretary of Defense (Comptroller), *National Defense Budget Estimates for FY 2000* (Washington, D.C.: Department of Defense, March 1999 and previous years).

[a] Includes $9.4 billion in emergency supplemental funding approved by Congress in May 1999 (PL 106-31).

the same time, the Clinton administration also was able to avoid making deep cuts in defense force structure and programs because of improvements in DOD purchasing power. The benefits of lower inflation for DOD are illustrated in table 2.6.

The final Bush defense budget plan (submitted in January 1993) projected that DOD budgets would total $1,782 billion during FY 1994–1999. In fact, actual DOD budgets totaled $1,672 billion,[61] $110 billion (6.2 percent) less. Lower inflation rates, smaller pay raises, and other positive developments during this period generated $112 billion in savings, $2 billion more than net total savings. These savings are for the most part outside the control of DOD decisionmakers, planners, and budgeters.

Internal DOD decisions resulted in net program budget reductions of $50 billion during FY 1994–1999, as shown in table 2.6. This was accomplished largely by halting production and deferring or restructuring new acquisition programs. At the same time, these savings were offset by $26 billion in supplemental funding and emergency funding requested by the Clinton administration and approved by Congress to pay for military contingency operations in Iraq, Bosnia, Kosovo, Somalia, and Haiti and military readiness budget shortfalls in FY 1999. Congress also added $26 billion on a net basis for programs—primarily related to military readiness—it wanted to pursue and support. The difference in program terms, as shown in table 2.6, between the final Bush defense spending plan and actual Clinton defense budgets is quite small—a $2 billion increase.[62] Chapter 3 shows that the actual defense budget levels of the 1990s were well below what was needed to support fully the forces envisioned in the 1991 base force plan,[63] 1993 BUR,[64] and 1997 QDR.

Nevertheless, improvements in DOD purchasing power enabled DOD to offset mandated nominal dollar budget cuts imposed by the OMB and to continue paying for its current programs on a real-dollar basis because prices for DOD goods and services had fallen enough. It is obvious that if DOD had had to absorb the $112 billion in reduced spending during FY 1994–1999 by making cuts in force structure, personnel levels, and acquisition programs, the QDR force would be very different today. This improved financial situation, however, was not large enough to pay for future force modernization, given the actual costs of maintaining military readiness and conducting military operations during the period 1993–1999 and the large and growing costs of the peacetime U.S. defense establishment—despite repeated attempts by the Clinton administration to streamline it and reduce its costs. In retrospect, lower inflation made it easier for senior defense officials to wait and defer painful cuts.

Tomorrow's Uncertain Economy

Today concern is growing that DOD budgets and long-range acquisition plans are overly optimistic in their assumptions about future inflation. The 43rd president and 107th Congress may inherit a defense budget that is severely underpriced in terms of inflation and may require considerable time and attention to rectify.

Figures 2.2 and 2.3 present the three-year moving averages[65] of annual price changes in DOD labor costs during FY 1982–1999 as well as currently projected changes for FY 2000–2005. The annual growth rate for both military and civilian pay has fallen sharply since FY 1982,

Figure 2.2
Trends in DOD Military Pay (3-year moving average)

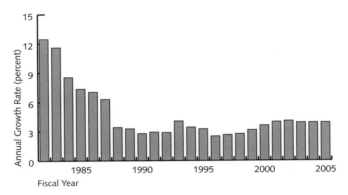

Sources: MSTI, based on data reported in Office of the Under Secretary of
Defense (Comptroller), *National Defense Budget Estimates for FY 2000*
(Washington, D.C.: Department of Defense, March 1999), 57.

largely in response to DOD downsizing and restructuring efforts that
began in earnest in FY 1987. A total of 680,000 active-duty military and
378,000 DOD civilian workers left DOD during FY 1990–1999 and were
not replaced. It would be difficult for pay to rise during periods in which
personnel levels fall. The February 1999 DOD spending plan for FY
2000–2005 assumed both military and civilian pay would grow at an annual steady rate of 3.9 percent during FY 2001–2005 as measured by a
three-year moving average. This is 0.9 percent higher than in 1998 and
reflects the 4.4 percent military pay raise proposed in FY 2000 and pay
raises of 3.9 percent thereafter.

From FY 1982 to FY 1999, the pay gap between military and civilian
personnel also widened. The chairman of the Joint Chiefs of Staff, Gen.
Henry H. Shelton, noted that the pay gap in FY 1999 ranges "from 8.5
percent to 13.5 percent," depending on which base year is selected.[66] In
their testimony before the Senate Committee on Armed Services in September 1998, the joint chiefs said unanimously that the pay gap is affecting military retention and recruitment rates and, therefore, steps must
be taken quickly to address this issue. The joint chiefs estimated that an
additional $5–$6 billion annually on a nominal basis would be needed
to close the pay gap. The February 1999 DOD military spending plan for

Figure 2.3
Trends in DOD Civilian Pay (3-year moving average)

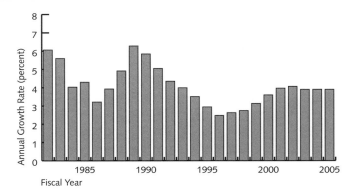

Sources: MSTI, based on data reported in Office of the Under Secretary of Defense (Comptroller), *National Defense Budget Estimates for FY 2000* (Washington, D.C.: Department of Defense, March 1999), 57.

FY 2000–2005 provided $5.6 billion (nominal dollars) on average.

Figure 2.4 shows DOD nonfuel purchasing costs measured as a three-year moving average. The rate of price increases gradually fell during the 1990s from an annual rate of 3.2 percent in FY 1990 to 1.2 percent in FY 1999. This reflected the decline in the inflation rate of the overall U.S. economy; the consolidation of the defense industry; and, most important, the absence of significant purchases of major DOD end items such as aircraft, ships, submarines, and tracked combat vehicles during the so-called procurement holiday. Senior defense officials currently expect prices to grow slowly during FY 2000–2005, reaching an annual rate of 2.1 percent in FY 2005. This growth rate, however, would be almost 58 percent below the inflation-rate average of 3.6 percent during the 1980s as measured between the 1982 and 1991 economic recessions.

Today's major question about inflation is: Are DOD prices ready to move up? The answer is especially important for DOD procurement accounts because, as DOD begins to procure major end items at the levels needed to modernize and replace the QDR force, planners need to know whether this new demand for equipment will result in a return to 1980s inflation rates or rates even higher. If inflation is higher than planned,

Figure 2.4
Trends in Prices of DOD Nonfuel Purchases (3-year moving average)

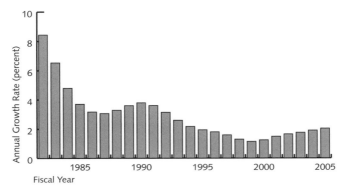

Sources: MSTI, based on data reported in Office of the Under Secretary of Defense (Comptroller), *National Defense Budget Estimates for FY 2000* (Washington, D.C.: Department of Defense, March 1999), 57.

purchasing power will fall as fewer dollars will be available to purchase less matériel. This, in turn, will slow the modernization and replacement rate of the QDR force and may lead to additional force structure reductions because of equipment shortfalls.

Because all DOD budget accounts are affected differently by inflation and DOD procurement accounts historically have been the major bill payer for unanticipated costs such as inflation, further losses in DOD procurement purchasing power would occur, especially under the flat budget topline envisioned by the 1997 QDR. Table 2.7 shows the effects of changes in the projected inflation rate on the DOD procurement budget during FY 2000–2005.

For example, as shown in table 2.7, the additional dollars needed during FY 2000–2005 should inflation rise by 25 basis points[67] across the period and across all DOD budget accounts would be $8.9 billion. If fully absorbed, this budget shortfall would act as a tax of 1.6 percent on the procurement budget. If the inflation rate should rise by 100 basis points (1 percent—slightly less than was experienced in the 1980s when DOD was buying large quantities of major end items), the budget shortfall would grow to $35 billion, a 6.4 percent tax on the DOD procurement budget.

Table 2.7
Effect of Inflation on DOD Costs, FY 2000–2005

Inflation Rate Forecast (percent) FY 2000 → FY 2005	Account	Additional dollars (in billions) required if inflation exceeds forecast rates by various basis point (BP) amounts			
		25 BP	50 BP	75 BP	100 BP
4.4 → 3.9	Military pay	1.4	2.8	4.2	5.6
4.4 → 3.9	Civilian pay	1.2	2.4	3.6	4.8
1.5 → 2.1	Other military personnel purchases	0.6	1.1	1.7	2.2
2.0 → 2.1	O&M purchases	2.3	4.7	6.9	9.2
1.6 → 2.1	Acquisition purchases	3.4	6.7	10.0	13.2
	Total 6-year adjustment	8.9	17.7	26.4	35.0
	Procurement reduction— if fully absorbed	1.6%	3.2%	4.8%	6.4%

Source: MSTI estimates.

Low inflation is critical to the future plans of the four military services. In developing long-range (25-year) acquisition plans, the military services, as is their custom, extrapolate on a straight-line basis across the planning period the inflation rate of the most recent year of the current spending plan (in 1999 that is FY 2005). DOD acquisition plans and programs therefore are currently built on an assumption that DOD procurement prices will grow no faster than 2.1 percent per year during the next quarter century. This is not realistic, however, given the inflation experience since FY 1945. Most important, the extrapolation of the strong economic and business results in 1998—arguably the best in many decades—creates an illusion that the QDR force and the military services' 25-year acquisition plans are indeed affordable over the long term.

Notes

1 For descriptions of the base force plan, see Dick Cheney, *Annual Report to the President and the Congress* (Washington, D.C.: GPO, February 1992); or Secretary of Defense, *1991 Joint Military Net Assessment* (Washington, D.C.: GPO, March 1991).

2 See, for example, Bill Clinton, "A New Covenant for American Security" (speech at Georgetown University, Washington, D.C., December 12, 1991); Les Aspin, "National Security in the 1990s: Defining a New Basis for U.S. Military Forces" (paper presented at the Atlantic Council of the United States, Washington, D.C., January 6, 1992) (Washington, D.C.: House Committee on Armed Services, 1992); and Les Aspin, "An Approach to Sizing American Conventional Forces for the Post Soviet Era: Four Illustrative Options" (Washington, D.C.: House Committee on Armed Services, February 25, 1992).

3 For descriptions of the BUR force, see Les Aspin, *Report of the Bottom-Up Review* (Washington, D.C.: Department of Defense, October 1993); or Les Aspin, *Annual Report to the President and the Congress* (Washington, D.C.: GPO, January 1994).

4 For descriptions of the QDR force, see Cohen, *Report of the Quadrennial Defense Review*; and Cohen, *Annual Report to the President and the Congress* (1998).

5 See, for example, Aspin, *Report of the Bottom-Up Review;* Edward L. Warner III, "Reply to the Coming Defense Train Wreck," *The Washington Quarterly* 19, no. 1 (Winter 1996): 120–124; and Cohen, *Report of the Quadrennial Defense Review,* x.

6 Dick Cheney, *Annual Report to the President and the Congress* (Washington, D.C.: GPO, January 1993), 3.

7 Cohen, *Annual Report to the President and the Congress* (1998), 2.

8 Cheney, *Annual Report to the President and the Congress* (1993), 1.

9 Aspin, *Annual Report to the President and the Congress* (1994), 16.

10 William S. Cohen, *Annual Report to the President and the Congress* (Washington, D.C.: GPO, 1999), 3.

11 Smaller-scale contingency events are reported by Hans Binnendijk and Patrick Clawson, who are editors of *Strategic Assessment 1995, U.S. Security Challenges in Transition* (Washington, D.C.: Institute for National Security Studies, 1995), 14–15; *Strategic Assessment 1996, Instruments of U.S. Power* (Washington, D.C.: Institute for National Security Studies, 1996), 127–142;

and *Strategic Assessment 1998, Engaging Power for Peace* (Washington, D.C.: Institute for National Security Studies, 1998), 153–168.

12 Shelton, "Posture Statement," p. 6.

13 Derived from data reported by Department of Defense, Washington Headquarters Services, Directorate for Information Operations and Reports, "Active-Duty Military Personnel Strengths by Regional Area and by Country, September 30, 1998."

14 McCain, *Going Hollow*.

15 Dennis J. Reimer, "Letter to Senator John McCain, September 25, 1998," in McCain, *Going Hollow*, 34.

16 Michael E. Ryan, "Letter to Senator John McCain, September 25, 1998," in McCain, *Going Hollow*, 37.

17 Binnendijk and Clawson, eds., *Strategic Assessment 1998*, 157.

18 General Accounting Office, *Military Operations: Impact of Operations Other Than War on the Services Varies*, GAO/NSIAD-99-69 (Washington, D.C.: GPO, May 1999), 2.

19 Ryan, in McCain, *Going Hollow*, 2.

20 Derived from data published in Air Force Association, *Air Force Magazine, 1991 USAF Almanac* 74, no. 5 (May 1991): 52–54; and Air Force Association, *Air Force Magazine, USAF Almanac 1999* 82, no. 5 (May 1999): 64–66.

21 Ibid.

22 Derived from ship and submarine commissioning and retirement dates published in Norman Polmar, *The Naval Institute Guide to Ships and Aircraft of the U.S. Fleet*, 16th ed. (Annapolis, Md.: Naval Institute Press, 1997).

23 Lieut. Gen. John Handy and Lieut. Gen. Gregory S. Martin, "Statements before the House Armed Services Committee Subcommittee on Military Procurement, Hearing on Aging Military Equipment," February 24, 1999.

24 Raymond Pyles, Laura Baldwin, Jean Gebman, Timothy Ramey, and Hyman Shulman, *Aging Aircraft: Implications for Programmed Depot Maintenance and Engine-Support Costs*, AB-237-1-AF (Santa Monica, Calif.: RAND, 1998).

25 Raymond Pyles, "Statement before the House Armed Services Committee Subcommittee on Military Procurement, Hearing on Aging Military Equipment," February 24, 1999 [emphasis added].

26 Krulak, "Statement of General Charles C. Krulak," pp. 3–4.

27 National Research Council, National Materials Advisory Board, Committee on Aging of U.S. Air Force Aircraft, *Aging of U.S. Air Force Aircraft, Final Report,* NMAB-488-2 (Washington, D.C.: National Academy Press, 1997), 3.

28 A good recent example of this issue is demonstrated in excerpts from a May 18, 1999, e-mail memo (reprinted in Elaine M. Grossman, "Air Force Finds F-16 Fleet is 'Broken, Unable to Reach Service Life,'" *Inside the Pentagon* 15, no. 20 [May 20, 1999]: 19–20) from the Air Combat Command's plans and programs directorate to air force headquarters and other major commands about the effects of aging on the F-16 fighter force, which numbers 1,470 aircraft:

> A. Our F-16 force structure is essentially "broken." The current Air Staff attrition model for the F-16 is optimistic, in that it uses a limited database that predicts artificially low attrition rates. The fleet is critically short in the Block 40/42 fleets. The Block 50's attrition fleet is short in the near term, and in post FY06. The currently proposed "F-16 buys" will not fix our attrition shortage. Our corporate Air Force needs to support a substantial buy of F-16 aircraft.
>
> B. Compounding the above problem is the fact that the F-16 has a projected shortfall in "airframe life." Current SPO predictions state that none of our F-16 blocks will last until the previously planned "8,000 hours" without substantial structural modification. Our F-16A's (required indefinitely for FMS training and test) are already being grounded. Initial indications are that funding is late-to-need SLEP'ing the pre-block 40 F-16Cs.

29 Clinton, "A New Covenant," 5.

30 Ibid., 7.

31 See the following by Les Aspin: "National Security in the 1990s"; "Tomorrow's Defense from Today's Industrial Base: Finding the Right Resource Strategy for a New Era" (paper presented at the American Defense Preparedness Association, Washington, D.C., February 12, 1992) (Washington, D.C.: House Committee on Armed Services, 1992); and "An Approach to Sizing American Conventional Forces for the Post-Soviet Era."

32 Aspin, "National Security in the 1990s," 1.

33 Ibid., 2.

34 Ibid., 6 [emphasis in original].

35 Aspin, "An Approach to Sizing American Conventional Forces for the Post-Soviet Era," 3.

36 Aspin, *Report of the Bottom-Up Review,* 4.

37 Bill Clinton, *A Vision of Change for America* (Washington, D.C.: White House, February 17, 1993), 22.

38 Ibid., 69–70 [emphasis in original].

39 Office of the Assistant Secretary of Defense (Public Affairs), "Bottom-Up Review," News briefing, September 1, 1993, p. 20 [emphasis added].

40 Cohen, *Report of the Quadrennial Defense Review,* vii.

41 Ibid., v.

42 Ibid., 25–27.

43 This program was approved by Congress in FY 1994.

44 This program was approved by Congress in FY 1993.

45 Based on data reported in Office of the Under Secretary of Defense, *Defense Manpower Requirements Report, FY 1998* (Washington, D.C.: Department of Defense, 1997 and previous years); and Cohen, *Annual Report to the President and Congress* (1999), 108.

46 Cohen, *Annual Report to the President and Congress* (1999), 149.

47 Secretary of Defense, *1999 Update Report of Defense Reform,* March 1999 <http://www.defenselink.mil/dodreform/1999update>.

48 William S. Cohen, *Report of the Department of Defense on Base Realignment and Closure* (Washington, D.C.: Department of Defense, 1998), 13–18.

49 National Defense Panel, *Transforming Defense, National Security in the 21st Century* (Arlington, Va.: National Defense Panel, December 1997), 84. The panel endorsed development of joint industrial activities, research and development (R&D) facilities, test ranges, and joint operational bases (e.g., joint air bases).

50 The 1988 BRAC round recommended the closure of 16 bases.

51 Ninety-seven bases were recommended for closure by all four BRAC rounds. Of those, two bases were closed in FY 1989. The final 20 are scheduled to close during the FY 1998–2002 period.

52 Cohen, *Report of the Department of Defense on Base Realignment and Closure,* i.

53 Cohen, *Annual Report to the President and the Congress* (1999), 167.

54 DOD's analysis focused on 259 bases (army, 74; navy, 103; air force, 76; Defense Logistics Agency, 6). For each category of bases, DOD defined a metric or a family of metrics. Each metric is a ratio of an indicator of capacity (maneuver base acres, facility square feet, etc.) with a relevant measure of

U.S.-based force structure (maneuver brigades, personnel spaces assigned, etc.) in 1989. For some installation types, this analysis examined more than one indicator. DOD then estimated future capacity needs by multiplying the 1989 metric value by the post-QDR force structure measure for 2003. The result is the amount of capacity required for future force structure, keeping constant the ratio of capacity to force structure that existed in 1989. DOD then estimated the increase in excess capacity by subtracting this estimate of capacity requirements from the amount of capacity that will exist after the BRAC of 1995. For details, see Cohen, *Report of the Department of Defense on Base Realignment and Closure,* 14–15.

55 Cohen, *Report of the Department of Defense on Base Realignment and Closure,* 11.

56 Ibid., ii.

57 Ibid., 15 [emphasis added].

58 Ibid., ii.

59 Cohen, *Annual Report to the President and the Congress* (1999), vii.

60 Reported in Otto Kreisher, "The Base Closure Flap," *Air Force Magazine* 81, no. 7 (July 1998): 63.

61 This includes $9 billion in emergency supplemental funding approved by Congress in May 1999 (PL 106–31).

62 This represents $50 billion in savings attributed to internal DOD actions offset by $26 billion in supplemental funding and $26 billion in congressional rescissions and reprogramming actions.

63 Dov S. Zakheim and Jeffrey M. Ranney, "Matching Defense Strategies to Resources: Challenges for the Clinton Administration," *International Security* 18, no. 1 (Summer 1993): 51–78.

64 Snider et al., *Defense in the Late 1990s.*

65 The average of the current year and the two preceding years.

66 Shelton, "Statement by General Henry H. Shelton," September 28, 1998, p. 3.

67 A basis point is 1/100 of 1 percent.

CHAPTER THREE

THE CURRENT PATH

We believe that the current QDR force, like the BUR force before it, is simply not affordable at the budget levels projected by DOD over the next 20 years (FY 2001–2020). We reach this conclusion by comparing the funding needed to support fully the QDR force (demand for funds) with the funding that will be available (supply of funds) over the same period. (See figure 1.3 and the budget forecast model on page 10.)

Our comparison revealed that DOD is faced with a budget shortfall of $88 billion in FY 2001 alone and $573 billion during FY 2001–2005. The costs of fully supporting the QDR force will require annual defense budgets equal to approximately 4.0 percent of GDP during FY 2001–2020, a 20-year period. In contrast, the Clinton administration projects that annual defense budgets will grow at a 1 percent annual rate during the next decade, from $270 billion in FY 2000 to $293 billion in FY 2009. Thereafter, if DOD budget levels continue to grow at annual rate of 1 percent during FY 2010–2020, the overall DOD budget will reach $327 billion by FY 2020. Given a growing economy, the defense budget will fall from 2.9 percent of GDP in FY 2000 to 2.4 percent of GDP in FY 2010 and, further, to 2.0 percent of GDP in FY 2020. The budget shortfall will grow accordingly, from 0.9 percent of GDP in FY 2000 to 1.6 percent of GDP in FY 2010 and, further, to 2.3 percent of GDP in FY 2020.[1]

In this chapter we examine in greater detail the factors that are shaping and influencing the DOD demand for money and the DOD supply of money. First we discuss the long-term economic outlook and federal budget outlook that define the overall economic and budget environment for DOD. We next examine and discuss long-term DOD O&S cost trends and issues. This will be followed by a detailed review of factors that determine both the supply of money and the demand for money for DOD procurement activities.

DOD TOPLINE NOT LIKELY TO GROW ANYTIME SOON

Long-Term Economic Outlook: Substantially Lower and Slower Economic Growth

Absent a clear and present danger, the 43rd president and the 107th Congress will find it very difficult to increase military spending substantially during their terms in office. Their actions will most certainly be influenced and shaped by the overall economic conditions (growth, inflation, interest rates, employment) of the nation and by the progress made between now and then toward reducing the federal debt and strengthening the financial condition of Social Security and Medicare.

Most important, their actions will take place within an overall demographic context in which the number of U.S. workers begins to decline as the baby-boom generation reaches retirement age and succeeding generations, reflecting lower birth rates, reach working age. The economic effects of this demographic trend will be a gradual and extended slowdown in the annual growth of real GDP. As this occurs, the burden imposed on the economy by budget shortfalls such as those projected for DOD or Social Security will become larger. This situation in turn may stimulate and intensify a guns vs. retirement check political debate in the first decade of the twenty-first century.

Evidence of a slowdown in real GDP growth is already apparent. Real GDP grew at an average rate of 3.6 percent per year between the economic recessions of FY 1982 and FY 1991. In contrast, real GDP grew during FY 1992–1998 at an average rate of 3.0 percent per year—0.6 percent per year less. Although real GDP growth is projected to be 4.1 percent in 1999, the latest 10-year economic projection by the CBO estimates real GDP will fall to 2.8 percent per year in FY 2000. And CBO further projects[2] real GDP will grow at an average rate of only 2.4 percent per year during FY 2001–2009—a view also shared by the Clinton administration in its latest economic forecast.[3]

Beyond FY 2009, the current Social Security and Medicare long-range economic forecasts, which are used by the two trustee boards for determining and evaluating the financial conditions of those trust funds, project further declines in real GDP growth. The April 1999 forecast projected the real GDP growth rate will fall from 1.8 percent per year in FY 2010 to 1.4 percent per year in FY 2020 and remain at that level through 2050.[4]

Long-Term Federal Budget Outlook: DOD Will Face Intense Competition for Fiscal Resources

Like their predecessors, the 43rd president and 107th Congress will be faced with the larger public policy issue of how best to balance the competing budget demands of the nation's financial security, social security, and national security programs. Financial collapse of one or all programs is possible, albeit unlikely, if no political consensus can be reached regarding changes in program costs, eligibility, and taxes. As time runs out, the need for a president or the Congress to act, or show results, will increase with each passing year and may come to dominate the nation's political agenda during 2001–2004. Such a situation obviously will influence and shape overall federal budget priorities as well as any effort to increase defense spending. The intense competition for fiscal resources among these three core program areas is already evident and will be profound over the long run.

Figure 3.1 depicts as percentages of GDP the actual spending and current projections of annual budget deficits or operating shortfalls for major programs comprising financial security, social security for the elderly, and defense in FY 1980–2030.[5]

The upper half of the chart shows the combined annual effects of the federal budget deficit,[6] net interest payments,[7] Medicare A trust fund operating deficit,[8] and the Social Security trust fund operating deficit.[9] The lower half of the chart shows the DOD budget shortfall described in chapter 1. The DOD budget shortfall, in this instance,

Figure 3.1
Projected Government Spending Shortfalls, FY 1980–2030

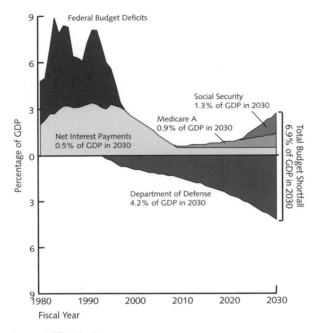

Source: MSTI estimates.

represents the difference between the cost of fully supporting the QDR force (see figure 1.3) and a defense budget that is continually maintained at a level equal to 3 percent of GDP during FY 1994–2030.[10]

The major budget demand trends and issues for each of these three program areas are briefly described and summarized below.

Financial security budget trends: Falling budget demands. As shown in figure 3.1, the overall financial security of the nation, as represented by the federal budget deficit and net interest payments, continues to show improvement across the period owing to higher revenue levels and a stronger-than-expected and still expanding U.S. economy. The United States recorded in FY 1998 a total budget surplus of $69 billion—the first since FY 1969.[11] According to the latest CBO 10-year budget projection, the federal budget is expected to be in surplus (not shown in figure 3.1) at least through FY 2009, assuming no changes in current policies or economic assumptions. The budget surplus in FY 2009 is projected to be $413 billion on a nominal basis—an amount that is slightly more than the entire DOD budget in FY 1985 (the last peak year of spending).[12]

Because of projected budget surpluses, net interest payments are assumed by CBO to fall as the need to issue new debt or refinance old debt diminishes. Federal debt held by the public will drop by $2.9 trillion on a nominal basis, from $3,720 billion in FY 1998 to $865 billion in FY 2009.[13] As a result, net interest payments also will drop on a nominal basis from $243 billion in FY 1998 to $71 billion in FY 2009. As a percentage of GDP, net interest payments in FY 2009 are expected to equal 0.5 percent of GDP—well below the 3.0 percent level that was experienced during FY 1985–1997.

In the event that projected budget surpluses are instead used to cut taxes or to fund program increases or new programs, CBO estimated that in FY 2009 net interest payments would increase by $123 billion;[14] net interest payments in FY 2009 then would equal about 1.1 percent of GDP. Figure 3.1 shows no further decline in net interest payments beyond FY 2009 because of current uncertainty about the outcome of the political debate over what to do with the projected budget surplus: cut taxes, increase spending, or reduce the national debt.

Social budget trends: Rising costs increase annual budget demands and threaten to deplete trust funds. Considerable public attention today is already directed at the major social security programs for the elderly, represented in figure 3.1 by the Medicare A[15] and Social Security.[16] The major challenge for this program area is the restoration and strengthening of the financial condition of these programs and, most important, the prevention of the depletion of trust fund assets.[17]

In terms of Medicare, medical expenses continue to grow faster than payroll tax receipts despite government efforts to contain costs. Medicare paid hospital and other medical care costs for 33 million aged and 5 million disabled beneficiaries in 1998, at an average cost of $3,460 per enrollee. It experienced operating deficits of $4 billion and $9 billion on a nominal-dollar basis in FY 1996 and FY 1997.

In April 1997, the Medicare board of trustees predicted that all assets of the hospital insurance trust fund will be depleted by FY 2001. To prevent this from happening, provisions were enacted, as part of the Balanced Budget Act of 1997 (PL 105-33), to reduce Medicare A expenditures by the amount needed to delay the hospital insurance trust fund depletion date until FY 2008.[18] As a result of stronger-than-expected economic growth, the Medicare board of trustees projected in April 1999 that the trust depletion date will be 2015.

Medicare Part A program expenditures will grow considerably in the next 30 years, owing largely to the aging of the baby-boom generation that will swell the ranks of Medicare beneficiaries. The Medicare board of trustees projected in March 1999 that the operating deficit will grow from $0.4 billion in FY 2007 to $323 billion in FY 2030 on a nominal dollar basis. The hospital insurance trust fund operating deficit will be 0.9 percent of GDP in FY 2030. This situation will affect 76 million beneficiaries.

Medicare A operating deficits, shown in figure 3.1, during FY 2007–2014 will continue to be eliminated by redeeming and using the assets of the hospital insurance trust fund. After 2015, when the trust fund is expected to be depleted, the Medicare A program would be prohibited by law from making monthly medical payments to eligible beneficiaries until Congress appropriates monies as part of the annual budget process. Thus the shortfall as shown in figure 3.1 is an unfunded expenditure under current law.

In terms of the Social Security program, the board of trustees in its *1999 Annual Report* projected:

- The first operating deficit for the disability insurance trust fund will occur in 2009, and all assets of that trust fund will be depleted by 2019. This date is four years later than reported in 1997. This situation will affect 11.8 million disabled workers and their families.
- The first operating deficit for the OASI trust fund will occur in 2024 (two years later than reported in 1997), and all assets of the trust fund will be depleted by 2036 (five years later than reported in 1997). This will affect 70 million retired workers and their families.

- The first operating deficit of the combined OASI and DI trust funds will occur in 2022. This date is nearly four years later than reported in the annual report of 1997.

In all three situations, the delay in the trust fund depletion date is attributed entirely to the better-than-anticipated economic developments of 1997 and 1998.

Finally, the annual OASDI trust fund operating deficits during FY 2022–2030 are expected to be paid with the redemption and use of the assets of the combined OASI and disability insurance trust funds. The combined operating deficit is expected to reach $482 billion on a nominal basis in FY 2030 and would equal 1.3 percent of GDP.

National security budget trends: Accelerating budget shortfalls will require large force structure reductions. The financial condition of national security, as represented by the DOD, will continue to deteriorate during FY 2001–2030 because budget levels—even when maintained at a level equal to 3 percent of GDP—are not high enough to pay for continued replacement, modernization, and operation of the QDR force, especially under conditions of a U.S. economy that is expanding more slowly. The DOD budget would be $280 billion in FY 2001—if maintained at 3 percent of GDP based on the March 1999 Social Security board of trustees 75-year long-range economic projection.[19] Such a defense budget would be $10 billion higher than the Clinton defense budget request for FY 2000. It would, however, still be $88 billion lower than the budget needed to support fully the QDR force. The QDR budget shortfall in FY 2001 would equal 0.9 percent of GDP as shown in figure 3.1. It would thereafter grow to 1.5 percent of GDP in FY 2010 and 2.6 percent of GDP in FY 2020. As indicated, the DOD budget shortfall would equal 4.2 percent of GDP in FY 2030.[20]

In summary, figure 3.1 shows dramatic improvements in the nation's overall financial security (federal budget deficit and net interest payments) as federal budget deficits cease and net interest payments fall because there is no need to issue new debt or refinance old debt, given projected budget surpluses. The red ink of the nation's finances will be replaced over the long term, however, by the red ink of the social security programs for the elderly (Medicare and Social Security) as their annual operating deficits grow. At the same time, national security budget shortfalls will grow larger and will exceed all nondefense budget shortfalls beginning in FY 2006.

The projected Medicare A and Social Security operating deficits, net interest payments, and DOD budget shortfall together will grow from 3.3 percent of GDP in FY 2000 to 6.9 percent of GDP in FY 2030. This represents a major economic challenge in peacetime. It also will be more difficult because of a smaller U.S. workforce that must support both a growing elderly population and a defense establishment badly in need of funds. The implications for DOD of these long-term trends underscore the importance of taking action sooner rather than later on financial matters relating to national security. Efforts to delay, defer, or engage in other kick-the-can-down-the-road actions serve only to undermine further the long-term financial posture and condition of DOD and to limit severely the choices available for future presidents and congresses. In addition, political and economic realities dictate that over the long term all program areas ultimately must be placed on sound financial footing.

DOD OPERATION AND SUPPORT COSTS CONTINUE TO GROW

DOD O&S spending pays for the salaries and benefits of all military and civilian personnel; the costs of operating and maintaining the armed forces; and the costs of operating and maintaining all military installations, facilities, and real property. It funds both the peacetime costs of the DOD establishment and the costs of military operations conducted by U.S. military forces.[21]

Current Trends

The February 1999 DOD spending plan for FY 2000–2005 projected that the O&S budget will decline by $3.4 billion, from $176 billion in 1998 to $173 billion in FY 2005 (see table 3.1).

O&S spending in FY 1998 accounted for 68 percent of the total DOD budget, and it is expected in FY 2005 to account for 64 percent of the total DOD budget. The decline in O&S costs is based largely on

Table 3.1
O&S Spending, FY 1998 and FY 2005 (FY 2000 dollars, billions)

Categories of O&S Spending	FY 1998	FY 2005	Change
Military Pay[a]	63.4	61.7	(1.7)
Civilian Pay	44.5	38.6	(5.9)
O&M Purchases[b]	68.5	72.7	4.2
Total, O&S	**176.4**	**173.0**	**(3.4)**
Share of DOD Budget[a]	68%	64%	—

Sources: MSTI, based on data reported in Office of the Under Secretary of Defense
(Comptroller), *National Defense Budget Estimates for FY 2000* (Washington, D.C.:
Department of Defense, March 1999).
[a] Excludes retired pay accruals.
[b] Includes family housing and military construction.

anticipated manpower reductions and related cost savings that are to accrue from success in planned DOD outsourcing, privatization, and competition efforts and in already planned streamlining and reengineering of DOD headquarters.

The prevailing assumption—inside and outside of DOD—for many years has been that O&S costs will not increase in real terms in the future. This assumption is contradicted by the recent actions by President Clinton to increase defense spending by $80 billion (FY 2000 dollars) over the FY 2000–2005 period; $61 billion of this (78 percent) has been allocated to pay for increases in military and civilian pay, military retirement benefits, personnel retention and recruitment budgets, and military readiness as measures for offsetting the effects of underfunding defense in the 1990s. The prevailing assumption is contradicted also by actual DOD cost experience observed during the past 40 years.

From FY 1960 to FY 1999, DOD O&S costs measured on a per capita basis for active-duty personnel grew at an annual rate of 1.6 percent (see figure 3.2[22]). This cost trend has continued during FY 1993–1999 despite concerted efforts by the Clinton administration to reduce and limit its growth. In fact, DOD O&S spending per capita accelerated slightly during the Clinton administration—from 1.4 percent a year during the Bush administration to 1.6 percent a year.[23]

Figure 3.2
O&S Spending for Active-Duty Personnel, per capita, FY 1955–2005

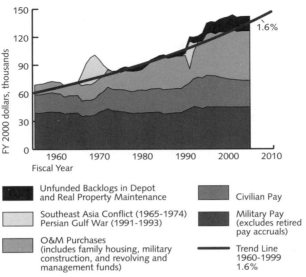

FY 2000 dollars, thousands

Fiscal Year

Legend:
- ■ (black) Unfunded Backlogs in Depot and Real Property Maintenance
- □ (light gray) Southeast Asia Conflict (1965-1974) Persian Gulf War (1991-1993)
- ▨ (hatched) O&M Purchases (includes family housing, military construction, and revolving and management funds)
- ▨ (gray) Civilian Pay
- ■ (dark hatched) Military Pay (excludes retired pay accruals)
- —— Trend Line 1960-1999 1.6%

Sources: MSTI, based on data reported in Office of the Under Secretary of Defense (Comptroller), *National Defense Budget Estimates for FY 2000* (Washington, D.C.: Department of Defense, March 1999 and previous years).

Slightly different annual O&S growth rates were observed during FY 1960–1999 for each of the military services: 1.9 for the army; 1.1 percent for the marine corps; 1.6 percent for the navy; and 1.5 percent for the air force. In terms of the major O&S cost elements and on a per active-duty military person basis, DOD military pay costs grew 0.4 percent a year while DOD O&M costs[24] grew 2.8 percent a year.

DOD spent $125,411 in O&S costs for each active-duty person in the force in FY 1998. The February 1999 DOD spending plan for FY 2000–2005 projected that O&S per capita spending will grow only slightly, reaching $126,300 by FY 2005. This expectation, however, is unrealistic for two reasons. First, budget shortfalls of $45 billion (nominal dollars) identified by the service chiefs in 1998 will still remain even after the spending increases proposed in the latest DOD military spending plan. Second, additional new budget shortfalls are likely to emerge as military equipment and facilities grow older. The question simply is:

When will DOD be forced to pay for these costs? Third, the budget increase of $74 billion (nominal dollars) for O&S[25] proposed by President Clinton reflects in part the cumulative effects of underfunding O&S accounts during the 1990s and of underestimating costs and overstating savings attributed to DOD management initiatives, defense reforms, and changes in defense business operations and practices. This situation has not changed in terms of FY 2000–2005. Nevertheless, in 1999, in real terms O&S spending per capita is 31 percent higher than the O&S per capita spending average of the 1980s.

If management efficiency and economy savings are not realized during FY 2000–2005, past DOD experience clearly demonstrates that additional reductions in DOD acquisition budgets will be forthcoming, most likely in the procurement accounts. These procurement reductions in turn will lead to additional delays in already postponed defense recapitalization and modernization efforts, deeper reductions in material readiness, and further increases in the age of U.S. military equipment inventories. As such, the cumulative effects of all of these outcomes will be to raise the military risks and human costs of future U.S. military operations.

The growth in DOD O&S costs during FY 1960–1999 is attributable to several major factors that are expected to persist for at least the next 10 to 20 years:

- Expanded personnel benefits, improved quality of life standards, increased demand for personnel-related support services, and the rising costs of benefits and services for military personnel, especially since the establishment of the all-volunteer force in 1973;
- Rising health care costs due to an aging military beneficiary population, greater demand for health care services and procedures, and expanded use of new and relatively more expensive medical procedures;
- Continued, and sometimes higher, maintenance and support costs for needed life extension, safety, and modernization upgrades of weapon systems that often are retained longer than their expected design lives owing to insufficient procurement funds for follow-on replacement systems;

Figure 3.3
O&S Budget Share Trends, FY 1955–2005

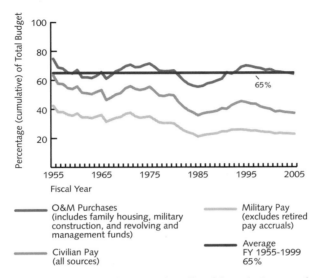

Sources: MSTI, based on data reported in Office of the Under Secretary of Defense (Comptroller), *National Defense Budget Estimates for FY 2000* (Washington, D.C.: Department of Defense, March 1999 and previous years).

- Higher maintenance and support costs of new, technologically sophisticated weapon systems compared with the maintenance and support costs of the systems they replaced, when examined on a total-force or total-life-cycle basis; and
- New demands—environmental programs, on-site nuclear weapons inspection activities, drug interdiction support activities, and Nunn–Lugar Cooperative Threat Reduction—placed on DOD for O&S funds.

Implications for Future Planning

The prospect of continuing growth in DOD O&S costs has important implications for future decisions about DOD budget allocations. The implications become greater in a budget environment that limits military spending to a constant level or flat topline, such as the 1997 QDR projection in which the defense budget remains stable at $266 billion per year for the entire FY 1997–2015 period.

Figure 3.3 depicts, as a percentage of the total DOD budget, annual budget allocations for major DOD O&S cost elements during FY 1955–2005. As indicated, DOD O&S spending averaged 65 percent of the total DOD budget during FY 1955–1999. This represents a 65:35 allocation ratio that is relatively stable across the period, moving within the 60–70 percent range.

Although O&S spending accounted for a relatively steady share of the total DOD budget, its composition changed with time. DOD labor costs as seen in figure 3.3 declined at a faster rate than O&M purchases. The long-term downward trends observed for both military and civilian pay were offset by a long-term expanding trend in O&M purchases. These trends parallel and reflect the long-term decline in force structure, equipment inventories and weapons stockpiles, and the number of military units as well as the transfer of work from the public sector to the private sector (contractor services) that has occurred during the past 50 years. Many of these changes were brought about by technological advances in modern weaponry, changing DOD organizational and management practices, and the end of the Cold War itself.

Nevertheless, although DOD payroll costs have declined over time, the February 1999 DOD military spending plan for FY 2000–2005 projected that payroll costs for a force of 1.37 million active-duty personnel, 837,000 reservists, and 637,000 civilians in FY 2005 will reach $100 billion and will account for 36 percent of the total DOD budget. Recent requests by the Joint Chiefs of Staff and the commanders in chief of U.S. combatant commands for higher military pay and better retirement benefits as measures for dealing with current military recruiting and retention problems will, if approved, raise future DOD payroll costs. In addition, unless DOD and Congress agree to reduce existing statutory personnel end-strength floors for each military service, DOD will have no choice but to pay a $100 billion annual payroll that will continue to grow. Consequently, any future budget adjustments stemming from a decline in the defense topline, changes in defense purchasing power, cost growth, or new military demands simply must be absorbed in their entirety by the remaining budget categories.

As a consequence of continuing growth in DOD O&S costs, future military spending plans that seek to maintain a constant budget topline

Table 3.2
Annual Budget Requirements of QDR Alternatives
(FY 2000 dollars, billions)

Categories of Spending	Near-Term Focus Path 1	Long-Term Focus Path 2	Balanced Focus Path 3*
O&S	178	162	167
Acquisition			
RDT&E	36	36	36
Procurement	52	68	63
Total, DOD	**266**	**266**	**266**
Budget Share (percent)			
O&S	67	61	63
Acquisition	33	39	37

Source: Derived from Cohen, *Report of the Quadrennial Defense Review*, 21–22.
* Path 3 was selected by the QDR.

or a constant O&S budget share will also—at the same time—need to identify measures for generating additional cost savings equal to at least the O&S cost growth rate of 1.6 percent per year. Failure to do so will lead to the continuation of the DOD practice in which procurement dollars migrate to O&S accounts to restore funding that was omitted owing to the chronic underestimating of DOD O&S costs or the overestimating of potential DOD O&S cost savings. In fact, the O&S cost trend indicates the O&S budget will grow to equal the entire FY 2001 DOD budget of $280 billion by FY 2023, or within 23 years. This prospect underscores the necessity and urgency for action today that will lead to and achieve major reductions in the physical plant of DOD military bases and installations and a fundamental transformation of the cost basis of DOD infrastructure services. Current efforts to create a revolution in business affairs within DOD therefore must be structured for determining the measures that, on a continual basis, will generate and increase savings equal to at least the current O&S growth rate.

A review of the projected annual budget levels and budget shares for each of the three QDR force options, presented in table 3.2, indicates that in 1997 senior DOD officials expected only small gains from efforts to create a revolution in business affairs and, therefore, little change in FY 1997–2015 budgets from the already established spending patterns. Together, the three alternative DOD force options considered by the 1997 QDR represented a narrow range of budget allocations—from a 67:33 ratio under path 1 to a 61:39 ratio under path 2. The fundamental resource challenge for the QDR was not the long-term affordability of desired U.S. military forces and capabilities; instead, the resource challenge was whether it was possible to adjust the allocation between O&S accounts and acquisition accounts because of the documented procurement-budget migration problem. In the end, the QDR recommended path 3, which is a 63:37 ratio. The QDR allocation ratio represents a 2 percent shift in budget share from what was experienced during FY 1955–1999 and is to be made during the next 18-year period.

It is critically important that DOD and Congress make budget and program decisions with the understanding and recognition that O&S costs have been growing and are likely to continue to grow for at least the next 10 to 20 years. Such recognition would lead to the development of more realistic cost projections and would allow for more realistic cost appraisals of current and alternative defense strategies, force structures, and investment programs.

DOD PROCUREMENT FACES TIGHT MONEY SUPPLY

DOD Total Money Supply Outlook

Total annual DOD spending measured in terms of total obligational authority has declined by $67 billion—20 percent—from $339 billion in FY 1992 (the last Bush budget) to $272 billion in FY 2000 (President Clinton's latest budget request). The February 1999 DOD military spending plan for FY 2000–2005 projected that the defense budget will jump to $280 billion in FY 2001, reflecting authorization for construction of a new aircraft carrier. Thereafter, the defense budget is expected to be $275 billion in FY 2002, $278 billion in FY 2003, $279 billion in FY 2004, and $281 billion in FY 2005. According to OMB's FY 2000–2009 10-year budget projection submitted to Congress, the DOD budget will continue to grow, reaching $293 billion in FY 2009. For the FY 2000–2009 decade, annual growth in defense spending will average 1 percent in real terms. This projection is in dramatic contrast to the May 1997 QDR projection that postulated that DOD budgets will remain flat or stable at $266 billion per year during FY 2005–2015.[26]

It is important to recognize that the $266 billion budget level does not represent the future budget requirements of the QDR force during FY 2003–2015. It represents instead a judgment about the defense budget levels that will likely be available during this period given the Clinton administration's long-range vision and budget priorities for the nation. The *Report of the Quadrennial Defense Review* stated:

> [T]he Department's plans are *fiscally responsible*. They are built on the premise that, barring a major crisis, national defense spending is likely to remain relatively constant in the future. There is a bipartisan consensus in America to balance the federal budget by the year 2002 to ensure the nation's economic health, which in turn is central to our fundamental national strength and security. The direct implication of this fiscal reality is that Congress and the American people expect the Department to implement our defense program within a constrained resource environment. *The fiscal reality did not drive the defense strategy we adopted, but it did affect our choices* for its implementation and focused our attention on the need to reform our organization and methods for conducting business.[27]

The emphasis placed on fiscally responsible plans reflects a major policy objective of the Clinton administration: the adoption of realistic projections of future defense budgets to ensure program stability in the out-years. The Clinton administration believes that program stability suffered greatly during the 1980s because, as Secretary of Defense William J. Perry wrote, there was a "fundamental disagreement between the executive and legislative branches regarding the resources that should be spent on defense."[28] As a result of that disagreement, defense budget plans routinely exceeded actual defense budgets. This situation led to large program instabilities in defense acquisition budgets and plans that ultimately resulted in cost overruns, higher production unit costs, program stretch-outs, and spending inefficiencies.

Because of its concerns about cost realism, the Clinton administration in one of its first acts commissioned a Defense Science Board (DSB) task force to determine if the defense program it inherited from the Bush administration was in fact properly funded. The DSB task force subsequently identified $21–$27 billion in potential budget shortfalls on a nominal basis across the FY 1994–1999 period related to defense management initiatives, weapon systems acquisition costs, environmental costs, and defense health care costs.[29] It also concluded a shortfall existed in the O&M budget but provided no estimate. In response to these findings, Secretary of Defense Les Aspin approved $15 billion of additional budget cuts to offset totally the budget shortfalls projected for FY 1994–1997. Although no public record exits today as to what specific actions were undertaken to eliminate the projected budget shortfalls in FY 1998 and FY 1999, as a practical matter these shortfalls were likely eliminated by subsequent DOD budget and programming decisions.

The prospects for realizing the president's proposed higher defense budgets are uncertain. First, the president's budget proposal is conditioned on the realization of the current size of the budget surplus. OMB's June 1999 budget projection estimates a 10-year total budget surplus of $2,926 billion (nominal dollars) for FY 2000–2009, of which $1,843 billion (nominal dollars) is the surplus for Social Security. The president's budget proposal calls for allocating the remaining $1,083 billion (nominal dollars)—the so-called on-budget surplus—as follows:

- $374 billion for strengthening and extending the solvency of the Medicare program;
- $250 billion for establishing universal savings accounts—a plan for targeted tax-deferred retirement savings;
- $127 billion for increasing resources for military readiness;
- $127 billion for ensuring sufficient funding for veterans affairs, environmental protection, health research, farm security, and protection of Americans at home and abroad;
- $74 billion for establishing a new trust fund for children and education; and
- $132 billion for other financing requirements, primarily for credit programs such as government direct loans or guaranteed loans.

If the FY 2000–2009 budget surplus shrinks because of tax cuts, higher program costs, or lower tax receipts caused by a slower economy, budgets will need to be reduced.

Second, the president's proposal for higher defense spending is conditioned first on the enactment of the administration's proposals for Social Security reform. President Clinton is strongly committed to "saving Social Security first" and his budget submission warns: "If Social Security reform is not enacted, discretionary spending levels [for defense] would be reduced to those assumed in the Balanced Budget Act of 1997 for 2001 through 2004."[30]

Adherence to the budget limits of the Balanced Budget Act of 1997 would eliminate entirely the $80 billion budget increase and force additional defense budget cuts that would be borne largely by the DOD procurement accounts—especially given the recent passage of the military and civilian pay raises and the higher costs of the military retirement system.

DOD Procurement Money Supply Outlook

Annual DOD procurement spending fell 36 percent in the first five years of the Clinton administration, from $70 billion in FY 1992 (the last Bush budget) to $45 billion in FY 1997. The DOD procurement budget rose to $46 billion in FY 1998 and rose again in FY 1999 to $50 billion. The February 1999 DOD military spending plan for FY 2000–2005 projected procurement spending would grow to $53 billion in FY 2000 and then jump to $61 billion in FY 2001 because of funding for construction of the navy's new aircraft carrier. Thereafter, the procurement budget will fall to $60 billion in FY 2002, grow to $63 billion in FY 2003, increase again to $64 billion in FY 2004, and increase to $68 billion in FY 2005.

These planned budget levels after much delay reach and exceed the $63 billion procurement goal[31] established in 1995 by the Joint Chiefs of Staff for attainment by FY 1998. Although the DOD procurement budget is projected to be $68 billion in FY 2005, it is not known publicly what DOD views today as the likely available DOD procurement budgets beyond FY 2005. The *Report of the Quadrennial Defense Review* stated that annual DOD procurement budgets will average $63 billion at least through FY 2015. This budget average represented the best-case estimate for DOD procurement.

The $63 billion best-case estimate is reasonable given historical patterns of defense spending. As discussed on page 78 and shown in figure 3.3, DOD O&S spending averaged 65 percent of the total DOD budget during the past 45 years, FY 1955–1999. Given an annual DOD budget of $266 billion, application of the historical 65:35 budget-allocation ratio for O&S and acquisition spending results in $93 billion annually for defense acquisition. Furthermore, if RDT&E spending is maintained at 11 percent of the total DOD budget—the level projected in the February 1999 DOD military spending plan for FY 2000–2005—the annual DOD procurement budget is estimated to be $64 billion; this is $1 billion more than the QDR best-case estimate. Past DOD spending patterns therefore indicate that, at a minimum, an annual DOD budget of $266 billion would be required to provide an annual procurement budget level of $63 billion. Such an estimate represents only the supply of money, however; it does not represent the demand for money based on the cost characteristics of QDR force (discussed on pages 86–89).

The 1997 QDR also contained a detailed analysis of the potential sources of instability (i.e., budget shortfalls) for FY 1998–2002 and an assessment of the implications of those sources of instability for budget requirements beyond FY 2002. On the basis of that analysis and assessment, the 1997 QDR stated that a maximum potential budget shortfall of $15 billion exists. In this worst-case estimate, the annual DOD procurement budget would fall to $47 billion.[32] This level of funding was considered to be clearly inadequate for carrying out the current military strategy. The *Report of the Quadrennial Defense Review* stated:

> . . . a procurement program of no more than $50 billion per year is clearly inadequate. Deterioration and obsolescence in equipment would erode long-term force structure and compromise the technological superiority of future forces. The concepts called for in Joint Vision 2010 could not be realized.[33]

Thus the DOD's own internal estimate of the break point or crash point for the QDR force was procurement budgets of only $52 billion annually.[34] Furthermore, this internal senior-level DOD assessment indicated that 25 percent of the stated procurement goal of the joint chiefs was considered to be already at risk financially on the basis of defense-budget assumptions used in 1997.

The 1997 QDR identified three specific potential annual budget shortfalls:

- $10–12 billion (nominal basis) for budget shortfalls resulting from the migration to other budget accounts of funding planned for procurement, owing to unprogrammed operating expenses,[35] unrealized savings from cost-reduction initiatives,[36] and new program demands;[37]
- $2–3 billion (nominal basis) for budget shortfalls in minor procurement and for unfunded modernization costs of major defense programs that were accumulated in the past and rolled over into a future procurement bow wave; and
- An unspecified amount for unavoidable costs related to managing the technical risk and program uncertainty inherent in large, complex, leading-edge DOD development programs.

To achieve and sustain the joint chiefs' procurement goal of $63 billion, the 1997 QDR presented a package of measures designed to mitigate and, if possible, eliminate documented potential budget shortfalls:

- $6–7 billion in savings to be derived from trimming forces, streamlining defense infrastructure, and adjusting modernization plans;
- $3 billion in savings to be derived from conducting two additional BRAC rounds in FY 1999 and FY 2001; and
- An unspecified amount in new funding to establish an acquisition program stability reserve fund in each military department that will be used to pay unanticipated costs of major defense development programs or activities.

DEMAND FOR PROCUREMENT MONEY IS LARGE AND GROWING

The future demand for money in terms of DOD procurement is determined by the number, types, models, technical nature, procurement unit costs, and procurement cost-growth experience of the items of military equipment that make up the desired military force. Realistic estimations of future DOD procurement budget demands for any postulated military force can be made through the use of three financial measures:

- Current replacement value,
- Annual depreciation cost, and
- Generational procurement unit-cost growth rates.

This estimation approach captures all the procurement costs for providing steady and continued modernization and replacement of a postulated military force and accounts for the effects of generational procurement-cost growth for all categories of equipment. This estimation approach often produces long-range projections very different from those prepared by the military departments, which routinely and consistently underestimate future procurement budget demands. These underestimations occur because long-range procurement budget plans of DOD and the military services often are based on

- approved DOD acquisition programs only; they therefore represent a partial or incomplete estimate of budget demands. Replacement programs or modernization programs not currently approved or simply deferred because of lack of funds by DOD acquisition executives are considered to be nonexistent and consequently cost-free now and in the future;
- overly optimistic assumptions about total procurement costs, production volume, delivery schedule, production rate, and production unit cost for major defense programs;
- unrealistic assumptions about the costs of acquiring additional technological capability or performance for new advanced weapon systems; and
- an erroneous assumption that less visible procurement end-items do not experience increases in costs over time.

The three financial measures used to estimate the future procurement budget demands of the QDR force are briefly discussed next.

Figure 3.4
**Estimated Current Replacement Value of 1997 QDR Force,
by Service and Equipment Category**

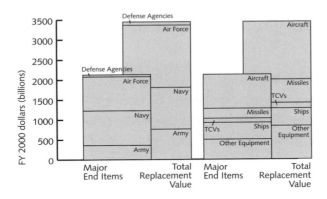

Source: MSTI estimates.

Estimated Current Replacement Value of the QDR Force

Current replacement value is the procurement cost of a postulated force at current prices, making use of available technology products.[38] It is generally computed for all inventory items on a one-for-one basis consistent with the latest acquisition objectives of the military services.[39]

As determined in 1997, the QDR force in FY 2003 will comprise approximately

- 15,682 aircraft (active and reserve),
- 304 ships and submarines,
- 41,553 army tracked combat vehicles, and
- 1.5 million missiles and munitions items.

These equipment inventories are considered by the secretary of defense and the Joint Chiefs of Staff to be the minimum levels that the military departments are to acquire, operate, maintain, and support during FY 1997–2015. The QDR force represents the desired military force end state for executing the current national military strategy during this period. The QDR force goals are intended to provide a common focus to DOD force development and resource allocation processes as well as a basis for evaluating the financial adequacy of current or alternative long-range defense budget plans and programs.

On the basis of the QDR force and equipment inventory goals described earlier, the current replacement value of the QDR force is estimated today to be $3,450 billion (see figure 3.4).

Of the $3,450 billion, $2,132 billion is estimated to be the replacement cost of major end items such as aircraft, ships and submarines, tracked combat vehicles, and missiles and munitions. The remaining $1,318 billion represents the current replacement value for equipment modifications, spares and repair parts, support equipment, and minor procurement and support items that are funded in the other procurement accounts of the military services' budgets.[40]

Estimated Annual Depreciation Cost of the QDR Force

Annual depreciation cost is the annualized procurement cost for the eventual replacement of an end item at the end of its operational service life. This cost is computed for each major end item (type, model, series) by dividing the current replacement value by the expected operational service life as estimated by the military service. Annual depreciation costs for all major end items are next summed to arrive at a total DOD annual depreciation cost.[41]

With this formula, the QDR force as defined earlier would need a procurement budget of $121 billion in FY 2000; see figure 3.5. In contrast, the president's procurement budget request for FY 2000 was $53 billion, an amount that is 56 percent lower. In terms of each military service, the procurement budget shortfall in FY 2000 was

- $20.6 billion (68 percent) for the army,
- $15.3 billion (41 percent) for the navy,
- $31.4 billion (62 percent) for the air force, and
- $0.9 billion (29 percent) for defense agencies.

The military services will absorb their budget shortfall in FY 2000 primarily by allowing the average age of their equipment to increase. For all of DOD, the average age of the QDR force would increase by nearly 7 months, assuming no change in equipment inventory levels. If such a shortfall were to persist in each year of the FY 2000–2005 five-year pe-

Figure 3.5
Estimated Depreciation Cost of QDR Force Compared with
FY 2000 Procurement Requests

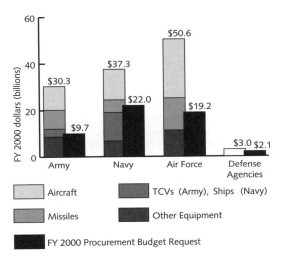

Source: MSTI estimates.

riod, the cumulative increase in the average age of the QDR force would be 35 months, or nearly 3 years.

Finally, dividing the current DOD replacement value by the annual DOD depreciation cost shows that the composite operational service life of the entire QDR force is estimated today to be 28 years. That is, the QDR force is made up of military hardware that must be replaced on average every 28 years.

Generational Procurement Unit-Cost Growth Rates

Annual depreciation cost is a useful financial measure for estimating the annual cost of buying today's forces or capabilities at current prices and available technology products. It does not capture, however, the additional costs often encountered in the past when next-generation technologies or capabilities were purchased. These additional costs, or cost premiums, pay for the acquisition of new technology products and use of advanced materials, components, and parts; new engineering, manufacturing, and production processes; and modern business practices.

Figure 3.6
Procurement Cost Growth — Tactical Fighters

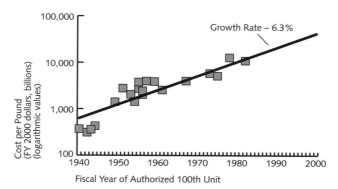

Fiscal Year of Authorized 100th Unit

Sources: 100th unit costs are derived from the following:
Department of Defense, *Program Acquisition Summary for FY 2000*
(Washington, D.C.: Department of Defense, March 1999 and previous
years); William E. Depuy Jr. et al., *U.S. Military Aircraft Cost Handbook*, TR-
8203-1 (Falls Church, Va.: Management Consulting & Research, Inc., March
1983); William D. White, *U.S. Tactical Air Power, Missions, Forces, and
Costs* (Washington, D.C.: Brookings Institution, 1974), 47.

To account for this cost-growth phenomenon, the annual depreciation cost for each major DOD weapon class is compounded over the
period under review by the generational procurement unit-cost growth
rate observed during FY 1940–1999.[42] Each major DOD weapon class
has its own cost-growth experience as shown, for example, in figures 3.6
and 3.7.

Nevertheless, on the basis of these cost histories, the composite annual procurement growth rate for total DOD is estimated to be 5.1
percent. This rate indicates that the annual DOD procurement budget
needs to double every 14 years to provide for steady and continued
modernization and replacement of the QDR force. That is, the DOD
procurement budget will need to grow from $121 billion (i.e., the depre-
ciation value) in FY 2000 to $328 billion in FY 2020. For the coming
10-year period (FY 2001–2009), annual DOD procurement budgets will
need to total $1.64 trillion or average $164 billion per year.

The composite procurement growth rate varies slightly by military
department: 5.4 percent for the army and 5.0 percent for both the navy
and the air force. This variation reflects the cost characteristics of the
QDR force—the interaction among inventory quantities, relative pro-

Figure 3.7
Procurement Cost Growth — Nuclear-Powered Submarines

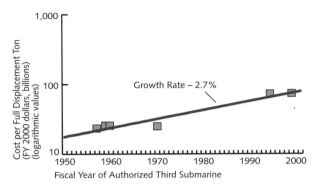

Sources: Third-ship costs derived from data reported in the Department of the Navy, *Fiscal Year 2000/2001 Biennial Budget Estimates, Justification of Estimates, Shipbuilding and Conversion, Navy, Budget Item Justification Sheet* (P-40), February 1999, and previous years of the same publication; William J. E. Shafer, *Cost Estimating Relationships for U.S. Navy Ships*, IDA Paper P-1732 (Alexandria, Va.: Institute for Defense Analyses, September 1983).

curement unit costs, past procurement cost-growth experience, and the expected service life of individual major end items.

The historical generational procurement unit-cost trends are intended largely as benchmarks of past DOD cost experience for the primary purpose of evaluating change and demonstrating progress. Their use is not intended to be predictive or to suggest that the United States is forever locked into, or doomed to suffer, the financial outcomes that are indicated by them. On the contrary, the intent is to increase awareness of the challenges involved; demonstrate the necessity and benefits of action; and stimulate new DOD management policies, practices, and actions that, if pursued over an extended period, would lead to better financial outcomes and desired military capabilities.

The generational procurement unit-cost trends also are useful for measuring the financial risks and opportunities underlying future DOD and military services' procurement plans and programs. The deviation from the trend line to a current planning estimate of a DOD weapon system represents the financial risks and opportunities associated with that program. When summed for all DOD programs, the deviations represent the overall financial risk inherent in DOD plans and programs.

The magnitude of these financial risks defines the soundness and cost realism of DOD long-range plans and programs in the context of past DOD cost-performance experience.

The use of these cost trends is not intended to prohibit a designated program manager from achieving program objectives. Instead, it is based on the experience of similar DOD weapon programs and is intended to bring realism to expectations about how many and what type of performance improvements can be achieved and at what cost.

There is some debate today about the relevance of generational cost-growth trends for estimating future DOD procurement costs. Some proponents of an RMA argue that these cost-growth trends are no longer relevant because future U.S. military forces will be composed of very different weapon systems as a result of anticipated breakthroughs in new, advanced military technologies and innovations. Once a new RMA-led weapon system family has been established, however, a new generational procurement-cost trend will emerge as the new equipment eventually is modernized and replaced in response to future advances in military technologies or changes in military threats. The unknowns today are the cost growth rate and frequency of replacement.

The likelihood of an RMA occurring before FY 2025 is already low and is becoming more remote given current projections about future overall DOD budget levels and directions of DOD's and the military services' long-range acquisition plans and programs. In fact, there is strong evidence to suggest that the current cost trends are likely to continue for at least the next 25 years. Although current service long-range visions of the next 25 years anticipate a number of new technologies, the services are still organized around large numbers of manned air vehicles, undersea vehicles, carrier battle groups, and heavy armored divisions. The future force characteristics the services are seeking reflect a continuation of current trends more than a break from them.

The 1997 NDP, for example, recommended that during 2010–2020 the U.S. military place greater emphasis on the following force characteristics:

- Systems architectures that enable highly distributed, network-based operations;

- Information-systems protection that protects against and identifies the origin of cyberattacks;
- Information operations that provide the capabilities to insert viruses, implant logic bombs, conduct electromagnetic-pulse and directed-energy strikes, and conduct other offensive electronic operations;
- Automation operations that speed mission-planning activities and military operations;
- A small logistics footprint that lowers the target signature of forces, lessens the strain on indigenous infrastructures, and reduces the demands on strategic airlift and sealift;
- Mobility that provides for better deployment and employment of forces as well as enhances force protection;
- Stealth that enhances the ability of forces to avoid detection and thereby contribute to tactical surprise;
- Speed that increases the rate at which U.S. forces can mobilize, deploy, set, act, and reset for any action—preemptive or reactive;
- Increased operational strike ranges that ensure the safety of U.S. forces and their ability to achieve desired effects from disparate locations; and
- Precision strike that enables the use of far fewer platforms with no loss in force capabilities and that limits collateral damage.[43]

The last five force characteristics certainly suggest a continuation of performance trends begun many decades ago. Although sometime in the future the military services may be willing to accept smaller but equally capable or better forces in relation to today's forces, none of the five force characteristics eliminates a current family of weapon systems.

In terms of potential cost savings, little information exits today to suggest that a future RMA force would in fact be cheaper to acquire or cheaper to replace and modernize over the long term than modernization and replacement of the existing QDR force. For example, although it may be true that shifting a substantial portion of U.S. aviation forces from manned aircraft to unmanned aircraft results in significant reductions in future overall defense procurement budget demands, this was not the cost experience observed during the transition from sailing ships to steamed-powered ships, diesel-electric-powered submarines to nuclear-powered submarines, piston engine to supersonic jet aircraft, or from the horse cavalry to mechanized infantry divisions. If an RMA force led in this direction, the long-term procurement shortfalls would grow substantially larger and call into question the long-term affordability of the RMA force.

Notes

1 OMB, *Budget of the United States Government, Analytical Perspectives,* 284.

2 CBO, *Economic and Budget Outlook: An Update* (Washington, D.C.: CBO, July 1, 1999), 12.

3 OMB, *Mid-Session Review* (Washington, D.C.: GPO, June 28, 1999), 8.

4 Board of Trustees of the Old-Age and Survivors Insurance and Disability Trust Funds, *1999 Annual Report* (Washington, D.C.: GPO, March 30, 1999), 58.

5 GDP percentages are based on actual GDP or latest government projections of future GDP as follows: For the FY 1980–1998 period, see OMB, *Budget of the United States Government, Fiscal Year 2000, Historical Tables* (Washington, D.C.: GPO, 1999), 169; for the FY 1999–2030 period, see Board of Trustees of the Old-Age and Survivors Insurance and Disability Trust Funds, *1999 Annual Report, Intermediate Projection* (Washington, D.C.: GPO, March 30, 1999), 175.

6 OMB, *Mid-Session Review,* 3.

7 CBO, *Economic and Budget Outlook: An Update,* 19.

8 Estimated for the FY 1999–2008 period by the Board of Trustees of the Federal Hospital Insurance Trust Fund, *1999 Annual Report, Intermediate Projection* (Washington, D.C.: GPO, March 30, 1999), 32; and estimated for the FY 2009–2030 period by the Board of Trustees of the Old-Age and Survivors Insurance and Disability Trust Funds, *1999 Annual Report,* 181.

9 Board of Trustees of the Old-Age and Survivors Insurance and Disability Trust Funds, *1999 Annual Report, Intermediate Projection,* 181.

10 Defense budgets that are continually maintained at a level equal to 3 percent of GDP are higher than the budget levels proposed in the president's FY 2000–2005 spending plan. This higher level of funding would reduce some, but not all, of the projected QDR budget shortfall during this period.

11 While recording a total budget surplus, the United States continued to post on-budget deficits that by law exclude Social Security and U.S. Postal Service revenues and expenses. CBO projects that an on-budget surplus of $14 billion on a nominal dollar basis will be reached in FY 2000, assuming no change in current policies or economic assumptions. On-budget surpluses also are projected for each year of the FY 2001–2009 period. By FY 2009, the on-budget surplus is expected to be $71 billion on a nominal-dollar basis. CBO, *Economic and Budget Outlook: An Update,* 14.

12 CBO, *Economic and Budget Outlook: An Update,* 14.

13 As a percentage of GDP (not shown in figure 3.1), federal debt held by the public would fall from 44.3 percent in FY 1998 to 6.4 percent in FY 2009.

14 This figure is based on CBO's January 1999 10-year budget projection, which projects net interest payments of $85 billion, or $14 billion higher than its July 1999 10-year budget projection. See CBO, *Economic and Budget Outlook: Fiscal Years 2000–2009* (Washington, D.C.: CBO, January 1999), 40.

15 The Medicare program discussed in this section and shown in figure 3.1 refers only to Medicare Part A, formally known as the Federal Hospital Insurance (HI) program. This is a nationwide health insurance program that pays for hospital, skilled nursing facility, and hospice care and some home health care services for the aged and certain people with disabilities. The Medicare A program is financed primarily by payroll taxes paid by workers and employers. The remaining Medicare programs, known as Medicare Part B (formerly Supplementary Medical Insurance [SMI] Trust Fund), are financed by annual appropriations.

16 The Social Security program, formally known as the Old-Age and Survivors and Disability Insurance (OASDI) program, consists of two separate trust funds that pay monthly benefits to workers and their families—Old-Age and Survivors Insurance (OASI) and Disability Insurance (DI). The Social Security program is financed primarily by payroll taxes paid by workers, employers, and the self employed.

17 Depletion of assets occurs when all trust fund assets are redeemed and used to pay over an extended period the annual operating shortfall. An operating deficit exists when annual expenses (the costs of benefits) exceed annual income (taxes and interest earnings) for a given year.

18 This was accomplished primarily by reducing Medicare A payments to most health care providers and, most significantly, by transferring payments of certain home health care services from Medicare's Part A to Part B. Part B relies on general federal revenues and insurance premiums to pay for the costs of this government program. Thus higher or lower spending levels in

Part B would be included and reported as part of the total federal budget deficit or surplus for a given fiscal year.

19 Under this projection, the GDP growth rate decelerates from 2.0 percent in FY 2001 to 1.4 percent by FY 2030.

20 The FY 2030 QDR budget shortfall would be 5.3 percent if DOD budget levels remain stable at $281 billion for the entire FY 2001–2030 period, using the same 75-year Social Security economic projection. If GDP grows at an annual rate of 3 percent for the entire FY 2001–2030 period, the FY 2030 QDR budget shortfall would equal 3.4 percent of GDP if DOD budget levels remain stable at $281 billion for the entire FY 1999–2030 period; the FY 2030 QDR budget shortfall would equal 1.7 percent if DOD budget levels were indexed to 3 percent of GDP.

21 In budget appropriations terms, O&S in this report refers to those programs, activities, or costs funded in the DOD military pay (less retired pay accruals), all civilian pay (regardless of funding source), O&M purchases, revolving management funds, military construction, and family housing appropriation accounts.

22 The growth rate in figure 3.2 is based on a regression equation:

$$y = (1.39e - 12) \times e^{.016065x}$$

The R^2 is .96. The trend line excluded the war years: Southeast Asia (FY 1965–1974) and the Persian Gulf War (FY 1991–1993). The regression line also excluded unfunded backlogs in depot maintenance and real property maintenance, which are shown for information only.

23 This observation is based on the difference between the extrapolation of a regression line fitted to the FY 1960–1993 period and a regression line fitted to the FY 1960–1999 period. The former represents the O&S cost growth experience from Eisenhower to Bush, and the latter adds to that trend the experiences of the Clinton administration.

24 This includes O&M purchases, all DOD civilian pay (including civilian pay funded in RDT&E and military construction accounts at different times during this period), military construction, family housing, and revolving management appropriation accounts.

25 This includes proposed increases in military retired pay accruals.

26 This represents the reported $250 billion budget level in constant FY 1997 dollars used by the QDR expressed now in constant FY 2000 dollars.

27 Cohen, *Report of the Quadrennial Defense Review,* v [emphasis added].

28 Secretary of Defense William J. Perry, on page 5 of an August 18, 1995, letter to Senator William V. Roth, in reply to Senator Roth's letter to Perry regarding "Anatomy of Decline," a critical study conducted by DOD employee Franklin C. Spinney.

29 In addition to its estimate, the DSB task force was presented with information that showed potential budget shortfalls ranging from $69 billion to $241 billion on a nominal basis for the FY 1994–1999 period. The GAO also identified potential budget shortfalls ranging from $8 billion to $88 billion over this same period. See GAO, *DOD Budget, Evaluation of Defense Science Board Report on Funding Shortfalls,* GAO/NSIAD-94-139 (Washington, D.C.: GPO, April 1994).

30 OMB, *Budget of the United States Government, Analytical Perspectives,* 284.

31 This represents the $60 billion procurement goal in constant FY 1997 dollars used by the QDR expressed now in constant FY 2000 dollars.

32 This is the QDR worst case of $45 billion in constant FY 1997 dollars used by the QDR expressed now in constant FY 2000 dollars.

33 Cohen, *Report of the Quadrennial Defense Review,* 62.

34 This represents the reported $50 billion break-even point in constant FY 1997 dollars used by the QDR expressed now in constant FY 2000 dollars.

35 The *Report of the Quadrennial Defense Review* specifically noted unprogrammed operating expenses involving depot maintenance, real-property maintenance, military construction, medical care, and the incremental costs of unplanned deployments and smaller-scale contingency operations.

36 The *Report of the Quadrennial Defense Review* specifically noted unrealized savings from recent DOD competitive outsourcing and business process reengineering initiatives.

37 The *Report of the Quadrennial Defense Review* specifically noted the need for additional funding to pay for 3 + 3 national missile defense, NATO enlargement costs, and sustainment of START I strategic force levels in the absence of the entry into force of the START II treaty.

38 The formula used to estimate current replacement value is

$$RV = ([N \times UC] \times P_1) \times P_2$$

where RV = replacement value; N = number of items in the inventory of the postulated force; UC = average procurement unit cost for three most recent budget years; P_1 = average ratio of major weapon system appropriation funding / new item procurement funding observed during FY 1974–1999; P_2 = average ratio of total service procurement funding / major weapon systems appropriation funding observed during FY 1974–1999.

39 There are three exceptions to the one-for-one replacement valuation: nuclear weapons, air refueling tankers, and long- and medium-range transport aircraft. They are valuated on a warhead or capability basis instead.

40 Other procurement accounts refer to the following procurement appropriations: Other Procurement Army (OPA), Procurement, Marine Corps (PMC), Other Procurement Navy (OPN), and Other Procurement Air Force (OPAF).

41 The P_1 and P_2 factors, presented earlier in the current replacement-cost formula, also are used in the formula to estimate the annual depreciation costs of modifications, spare and repair parts, support equipment, and other procurements.

42 This typically is accomplished by determining the trend of unit cost when moving from one generation to the next at the same point in the production cycle (e.g., 100th aircraft unit cost, 3rd ship cost, or 1,000th missile unit cost).

43 National Defense Panel, *Transforming Defense*, 44–45.

CHAPTER FOUR

AFFORDABLE FORCES

DOD PROCUREMENT BUDGETS WILL NEED TO AVERAGE $164 BILLION ANNUALLY DURING FY 2001–2010 to provide for steady and continued modernization and replacement of the QDR force on the basis of the cost characteristics (inventory levels, current procurement unit costs, expected service lives, and generational procurement unit-cost growth experiences) of the QDR force.[1] This annual DOD procurement budget will fall to $111 billion if the costs of strategic bombers, aerial tankers, strategic submarines, and all nuclear weapons are excluded. Such an estimate is consistent with current DOD acquisition plans, in which no new purchases of these items are anticipated during the first decade of the twenty-first century.

At some future date, however, these deferred purchases of strategic weapon systems will have to be made up to provide a constant ready force over the expected lifetime of QDR force. It is important therefore to remember that, by FY 2010, 20 years will have passed since the last authorization to buy a strategic missile submarine and 17 years since the last authorization to buy a strategic bomber. At the end of the next decade, RDT&E decisions about the future of these forces will be needed. Those decisions in turn will have major implications for the future size of DOD acquisition budgets.

Nevertheless, the $164 billion average annual DOD procurement budget demands will far exceed the projected supply of procurement money during FY 2001–2010. If annual DOD spending is limited to $266 billion, the 1997 QDR projected annual procurement budgets will

Table 4.1
DOD Procurement Bow Wave (FY 2000 dollars, billions)

Spending	FY 1993-2000	FY 2001–2005	FY 2006–2020
Steady State Spending	819	705	3552
Prior Deferred Spending	0	426	815
Budget Demands	819	1131	4367
Available Monies	393	316	1020
Cumulative Deferred Spending	426	815	3347
Budget Demands divided by Steady State Spending	100%	160%	123%

Source: MSTI estimates.

range from $47 billion in the worst case to $63 billion in the best case. Accordingly, money demand in DOD will exceed money supply in DOD during this period by a ratio of 3.5:1 in the worst case and 2.6:1 in the best case. Without additional reductions in QDR inventory levels, the military departments will have no choice but to defer spending again and again. Such actions in turn will add to the size of the future defense procurement bow wave. See table 4.1.

The military departments already deferred $426 billion of procurement purchases during FY 1993–2000. These deferred purchases accounted for 52 percent of the procurement budget demand during this period. Under the February 1999 military spending plan for FY 2000–2005, DOD plans to defer during FY 2001–2005 another $389 billion ($705 billion minus $316 billion). Cumulative deferred purchases therefore will total $815 billion by FY 2005 and will be rolled over into the future DOD procurement bow wave. These deferred purchases in turn raise future procurement budget levels—if QDR forces are to be maintained. For example, if the $815 billion cumulative deferred purchases are added to the procurement demand for the next 15-year period (FY 2006–2020), the procurement budget will be $4,367 billion or 23 percent higher than if no deferrals been made since FY 1993. That is, the demand for procurement dollars in the FY 2006–2020 15-year period will grow from $3,552 billion ($231 billion per year) to $4,367 billion

Figure 4.1
Annual Affordability Assessment, DOD, FY 2001–2010

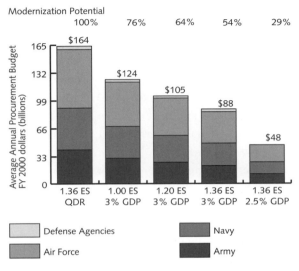

Source: MSTI estimates.
* ES refers to active-duty personnel end strength (millions).

($291 billion per year) when prior year spending deferrals are included. By continuing to kick the can down the road, the military departments will, in effect, create a situation in which they require $4,367 billion in procurement dollars in FY 2006–2020—if the QDR force is to be maintained beyond FY 2020.

Regarding money supply, if DOD maintains procurement budgets at $68 billion (the current projection for FY 2005),[2] by 2020 the procurement bow wave (deferred spending) will reach $3,347 billion, given the spending deferrals of FY 1993–2020. At some future date the accumulation of prior-year unfunded purchases will result in a procurement due bill that can never be paid. Force structure, equipment inventories, and munitions stockpiles therefore will shrink at the rate military equipment is finally retired because of physical obsolescence or uneconomic costs. As this occurs, U.S. military forces will lose their credibility both at home and abroad regarding their size, age, and technological capabilities for carrying out the national military strategy.

The magnitude of possible force reductions and force restructuring options is illustrated in figure 4.1, which is arranged according to different overall DOD budget toplines and active-duty personnel end-strength levels. To provide for continued modernization and replacement of the QDR force during FY 2001–2010, described on page 10 and depicted in the bar on the far left of the chart, DOD procurement budgets will need to average $164 billion annually. This would support an active-duty end strength (ES) of 1.37 million personnel. It also would provide for a new and fully modernized full-strength QDR force; this is represented by the modernization potential score of 100 percent displayed above the bar.

The next three bars of figure 4.1 provide possible force restructuring options during FY 2001–2010 for overall DOD budget toplines maintained at a level equal to 3 percent of GDP[3] but with three different active-duty personnel end-strength levels (in millions). As indicated by the fourth bar from the left, the O&S costs associated with the current QDR active-duty personnel end strength of 1.37 million would leave only $88 billion available for annual procurement. This level of funding would be adequate for modernization and replacement of 54 percent of the QDR force. Unless assigned equipment could continue to operate—physically and economically—beyond its projected operational service life, force levels would fall eventually by 46 percent.[4]

If military departments seek to maintain the QDR force structure, 54 percent of the equipment would be modern and the remaining 46 percent would be operating beyond its expected service life—if the military departments were able to find ways of extending the service of equipment and funded the life extensions in a timely manner. This older force in turn would lead to higher O&M budgets as dollars would be diverted from procurement budgets to pay for the additional maintenance. The loss of additional procurement dollars would contribute to another round of delays in force modernization.

The second and third bars from the left show that the services alternatively could achieve 76 percent or 64 percent of their modernization potential by reducing active-duty personnel end-strength levels to 1.0 million (bar 2) or 1.2 million (bar 3). These force-restructuring alternatives demonstrate potential trade-offs between manpower and equipment.

Table 4.2
QDR Force Composition and Replacement Costs — Aircraft

Service	Inventory	AURC*
Army	5,796	22
Navy and Marine Corps	4,059	84
Air Force	5,827	117
Total, DOD	**15,682**	**69**

Source: MSTI estimates.
* AURC: average unit replacement cost for FY 2001–2010 (in FY 2000 dollars, millions).

Finally, the fifth bar shows the outcome in light of current financial trends. In this instance, the overall DOD budget topline is maintained during the decade at a level equal to 2.5 percent of GDP. At this overall budget level, the O&S costs associated with the current QDR active-duty end strength of 1.37 million would now leave only $48 billion for annual procurement, a level just above the $47 billion QDR worst-case estimate and well below the QDR break point of $52 billion. This level of procurement funding would be sufficient only to modernize and replace 29 percent of the QDR force.

Figures 4.2, 4.3, and 4.4 present the effects of the potential shortfall on QDR inventory levels for aircraft, ships and submarines, and army tracked combat vehicles.

DOD AIRCRAFT

The combined total QDR aviation force (all services, active and reserve) consists of 15,682 aircraft (see table 4.2). Figure 4.2 shows that an annual production rate of 578 aircraft would be required to maintain this inventory level over the long term, given the expected service lives of aircraft as determined by the military departments. Therefore, as shown by the bar on the far left of the figure, the procurement budget for QDR aviation forces would need to average $68 billion annually during FY 2001–2010. In contrast, the FY 2000 DOD budget request to Congress proposed spending $19 billion from aircraft procurement accounts, producing 148 new-production aircraft.[5]

Figure 4.2
Annual Affordability Assessment, DOD Aircraft (active and reserve)
FY 2001–2010

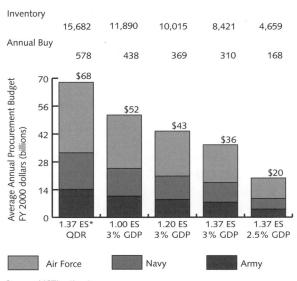

Source: MSTI estimates.

* ES refers to active-duty personnel end strength (millions).

As shown in the fourth bar from the left, an overall DOD topline that is maintained at a level equal to 3 percent of GDP and structured to support an active-duty end strength of 1.37 million during FY 2001–2010 would leave available only $36 billion annually for aircraft procurement. This funding level would lead to a substantial drop in the annual aircraft production rate, from 578 to 310. Aircraft inventories eventually would fall from 15,682 to 8,421.

With no change in the overall DOD budget level, smaller active-duty end-strength levels of 1.2 million (bar 3) or 1.0 million (bar 2) would make available more dollars for aircraft procurement. The average annual aircraft procurement budget would grow from $36 billion to $43 billion and $52 billion, respectively. A $43 billion annual aviation procurement budget would be adequate to support an annual production rate of 369 aircraft. This in turn would sustain an inventory of 10,015 aircraft. A $52 billion annual aviation procurement budget

Table 4.3
QDR Force Composition and Replacement Costs —
Ships and Submarines

Class	Inventory	AURC*
Strategic Missile Submarines (SSBN)	14	3,998
Attack Submarines (SSN)	50	2,800
Aircraft Carriers (CV, CVN)	12	6,032
Surface Combatants (CG, DD, DDG, FFG)	120	1,491
Amphibious Warfare Forces (LHA, LHD, LPD, LSD, LST)	36	1,188
Combat Logistics Forces (AE, AFS, AOE, AO, ADC)	33	586
Mine Warfare Forces (MCM, MHC)	16	367
Support Ships (AS, ATF, AGOS, AGF, LCC, ARS)	23	484
Total	**304**	**1,782**

Source: MSTI estimates.
* AURC: average unit replacement cost for FY 2001–2010 (in FY 2000 dollars, millions).

would be adequate to support an annual production rate of 438 aircraft. This in turn would sustain an inventory of 11,890 aircraft.

Finally, as depicted by the bar on the far right, an overall annual DOD budget maintained at a level equal to 2.5 percent of GDP and structured to support 1.37 million active-duty personnel would leave $20 billion for aircraft procurement. This budget level would be sufficient to support an annual production rate of 168 aircraft. This rate in turn would sustain a total DOD aircraft inventory of 4,659 aircraft—a level slightly higher than the QDR aircraft inventory for the navy and marines only.

DOD SHIPS AND SUBMARINES

The QDR naval forces consist of 304 ships and submarines (see table 4.3). Figure 4.3 shows that an annual shipbuilding rate of 8 is required to maintain a fleet of 304 ships and submarines over the long term given

Figure 4.3
Annual Affordability Assessment, DOD Ships and Submarines
FY 2001–2010

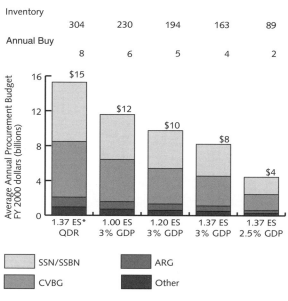

Source: MSTI estimates.
* ES refers to active-duty personnel end strength (millions).

their expected service lives as determined by the navy. As shown in the first bar on the left side of the chart in figure 4.3, during FY 2001–2010 the navy would need an average annual shipbuilding and conversion, navy (SCN) budget of $15 billion to provide for continued modernization and replacement of QDR naval forces. In contrast, the navy requested authorization to build six ships and approval of $6.7 billion SCN funding for FY 2000.

As shown in the fourth bar from the left, an overall annual DOD budget that is maintained at a level equal to 3 percent of GDP and structured to support an active-duty end strength of 1.37 million during FY 2001–2010 would leave only $8 billion available for SCN on an annual basis. This would lead to a drop from eight to four in the annual shipbuilding rate. The size of the naval fleet would eventually fall from 304 to 163.

Table 4.4
QDR Force Composition and Replacement Costs —
Army Tracked Combat Vehicles

Class	Inventory	AURC*
Tanks	7,991	7.16
Fighting Vehicles and Armored Personnel Carriers	29,610	2.41
Artillery, Towed	1,928	1.18
Artillery, Self-Propelled	2,024	1.60
Total	**41,553**	**3.23**

Source: MSTI estimates.

* AURC: average unit replacement cost for FY 2001–2010 (in FY 2000 dollars, millions).

With no change in the overall DOD topline, a smaller active-duty end-strength level of $1.2 million (bar 3) or 1.0 million (bar 2) would make available additional SCN dollars. The average annual SCN budget would increase from $8 billion to $10 billion and $12 billion, respectively. A $10 billion annual SCN budget would be adequate for supporting an annual shipbuilding rate of five ships or submarines and therefore would sustain a naval fleet of 194 ships and submarines. A $12 billion annual SCN budget would be adequate for supporting an annual shipbuilding rate of 6 ships or submarines and consequently would sustain over the long term a naval fleet of 230 ships and submarines.

Finally, an overall annual DOD budget level maintained at a level equal to 2.5 percent of GDP and structured to support 1.37 million active-duty personnel (the far-right bar) would leave only $4 billion for SCN on annual basis. Such a budget level would be adequate to support an annual shipbuilding rate of only two ships or submarines, a rate that would sustain only 89 ships and submarines over the long term.

ARMY TRACKED COMBAT VEHICLES

The combined (active and reserve) army QDR tracked combat vehicles force consists of 41,553 vehicles (see table 4.4). Figure 4.4 shows that an annual production rate of 1,039 vehicles is required over the long term to maintain this force level. As shown in the first bar on the left side of

Figure 4.4
Annual Affordability Assessment, Army Tracked Combat Vehicles FY 2001–2010

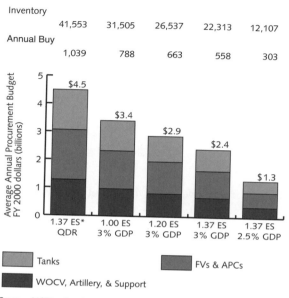

Inventory
41,553   31,505   26,537   22,313   12,107

Annual Buy
1,039   788   663   558   303

Average Annual Procurement Budget FY 2000 dollars (billions)

$4.5 $3.4 $2.9 $2.4 $1.3

1.37 ES*   1.00 ES   1.20 ES   1.37 ES   1.37 ES
QDR   3% GDP   3% GDP   3% GDP   2.5% GDP

Tanks   FVs & APCs

WOCV, Artillery, & Support

Source: MSTI estimates.
* ES refers to active-duty personnel end strength (millions).

the chart in figure 4.4, the annual procurement budget for army tracked combat vehicles during FY 2001–2010 would need to average $4.5 billion. Contrast this with the army budget request in FY 2000 in which $1.4 billion was sought and 12 new-production vehicles were requested.

As shown in the fourth bar from the left, an overall annual DOD budget that is maintained at a level equal to 3 percent of GDP and structured to support an active-duty end strength of 1.37 million during FY 2001–2010 would leave only $2.4 billion available for tracked combat vehicles on an annual basis. This would lead to a substantial decline in the vehicle production rate, from 1,039 to 558. Inventories would fall eventually from 41,553 to 22,313 vehicles.

With no changes in the overall DOD topline, a smaller active-duty end strength of 1.2 million (bar 3) or 1.0 million (bar 2) would make available more procurement dollars for army tracked combat vehicles.

The average annual army tracked combat vehicle procurement budget would grow from $2.4 billion to $2.9 billion and $3.4 billion, respectively. A $2.9 billion annual procurement budget would be adequate to support an annual production rate of 663 vehicles. This rate in turn would sustain an inventory of 26,537. A $3.4 billion annual procurement budget would be adequate to support an annual production rate of 788 vehicles that, in turn, would provide for an inventory of 31,505.

Finally, an overall annual DOD budget maintained at a level equal to 2.5 percent of GDP and structured to support 1.37 million active-duty personnel (bar on the far right) would leave $1.3 billion for army tracked combat vehicles. This budget level would be adequate for supporting an annual production rate of 303 vehicles and, consequently, would be enough to sustain over the long term an inventory of only 12,107 tracked combat vehicles.

Notes

1 CBO has presented for the first time its estimate of the steady state procurement outlook for current DOD force structure; CBO estimated a DOD procurement budget of $90 billion is needed. This is lower than our estimate because CBO assumes DOD will keep its major weapon systems longer. See statement of Lane Pierrot, Senior Analyst, National Security Division, Congressional Budget Office, before the Subcommittee on Military Procurement of the House Committee on Armed Services, February 24, 1999; and CBO, *An Analysis of the President's Budgetary Proposals for Fiscal Year 2000*, 49–50.

2 This is $5 billion higher than the 1997 QDR projection for 1997–2015.

3 For illustrative purposes, real GDP is assumed to grow 3.0 percent per year for these three alternatives.

4 The actual timing of the reductions will be determined by the actual age distribution of military equipment.

5 This includes funding reported in the following DOD appropriation categories: Aircraft Procurement Army (APA), Aircraft Procurement Navy (APN), Aircraft Procurement Air Force (APAF), and aircraft budget subcategories of the National Guard and reserve equipment procurement appropriation.

CHAPTER FIVE

KEY DECISIONS

THE 43RD PRESIDENT AND 107TH CONGRESS MUST MAKE TWO KEY DECISIONS IN THE FIRST 100 DAYS. First, they must balance the manpower, modernization, and budget demands of U.S. military forces. Strategy, forces, and budgets must be reconciled, or military capabilities will be lost during their terms in office or immediately thereafter. U.S. military forces must be made affordable over the long run. If not, U.S. national security strategy and national military strategy will be viewed at home and overseas as no longer credible.

Second, the 43rd president and 107th Congress must decide on the forces and capabilities that will replace current U.S. military forces and capabilities. These decisions must be shaped and formulated by a new DOD force modernization strategy and acquisition program that must define and specify the timing, technology character, and composition of the force that will replace the QDR force. The program also must address aging and retirement issues that arise from the fact that U.S. military forces are reaching the end of their operational service life. The new acquisition strategy and program, at a minimum, must

- assign a higher resource priority to measures that extend and stretch the service life of critical military capabilities during the transition period to ensure availability to the national command authority; and
- define the speed at which future force modernization should proceed: What kinds of improvements in capabilities are affordable and represent the best use of defense dollars?

The new DOD force modernization strategy and acquisition program must be affordable over the long run; affordability must be based on realistic assessments of defense costs and defense budgets likely to be available. The new DOD acquisition strategy and program must serve to refocus and energize DOD efforts, from the military laboratories to operational units, about what is needed and when as well as how to leverage fully and continually scarce defense resources.

NEW STRATEGY–RESOURCES BALANCE

The first key action for the 43rd president and 107th Congress must be to balance the manpower, modernization, and budget demands of the desired levels of U.S. military forces (personnel and equipment) and then maintain them because at the beginning of the twenty-first century, the manpower, modernization, and budget demands of desired U.S. military forces will be greatly out of balance. DOD budget levels projected during FY 2001–2010 are too low to support the continued modernization, replacement, and operation of the QDR force, with its great size and technological sophistication, and at the same time the military pay, benefits, quality of life, and training costs of a 1.37 million active-duty military force.

The range of possible options for consideration is illustrated in figure 5.1, which displays U.S. military forces in terms of two dimensions. The x axis displays the size of the active-duty component, measured in terms of active-duty end strength. The y axis displays the relative amount of modernized military equipment assigned to U.S. military forces, measured as the ratio of available procurement spending over the required steady state procurement spending for the QDR force for FY 2001–2010. The diagonal black lines represent the size of the overall defense budget in terms of a fixed share of GDP.

The defense budget in FY 2002, in figure 5.1, would have to be $380 billion to support fully the QDR force, indicated by the uppermost horizontal gray line. Such a budget level would be $105 billion higher than that proposed in the February 1999 DOD spending plan for FY 2000–2005 and would equal 3.9 percent of GDP. Thus defense budgets smaller than 3.9 percent of GDP will require during the FY 2001–2010 decade

Figure 5.1
DOD Personnel, Modernization, and Budget Options, FY 2002–2010

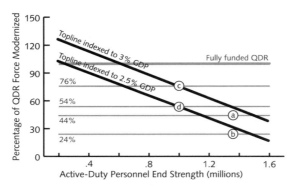

Source: MSTI estimates.

a   1.37 million active-duty force; 2.8 percent of GDP spent on defense
    (FY 2002)
b   1.37 million active-duty force; 2.4 percent of GDP spent on defense
    (FY 2009)
c   1 million active-duty force; 3 percent of GDP (indexed) spent on defense
d   1 million active-duty force; 2.5 percent of GDP (indexed) spent on defense

additional force structure and manpower reductions, given the current cost characteristics of the QDR force.

The president's budget projection for FY 2002 is the circle labeled a, in which the United States wants to spend approximately $275 billion (2.8 percent of its GDP) on defense and maintain an active-duty force of 1.37 million. If defense spending was maintained at this GDP level for FY 2001–2010, it would leave, as shown in figure 5.1, enough procurement dollars to pay for modernization and replacement of only 44 percent of the QDR force equipment. Unless assigned equipment could continue to operate beyond its projected service life, in both physical and economic terms, the military services eventually would see their force levels fall by as much as 56 percent as military equipment reached the end of useful service or economic life and would be retired. Equipment inventories subsequently would fall because replacement units would not be funded. A 56 percent reduction of the QDR forces would clearly call into question the capabilities of the U.S. armed forces to carry out the national military strategy.

By FY 2009, DOD may in fact be in the situation of circle b in figure 5.1, with total DOD spending having fallen to 2.4 percent of GDP and the active-duty force being maintained at 1.37 million. The reduction in overall DOD spending coupled with no change in the costs of the active-duty force would result in lower levels of funding for DOD procurement that would pay for only 24 percent of the QDR force modernization. This eventually would lead to a 76 percent reduction in QDR force levels, a level that would also be inadequate for carrying out the national military strategy.

Two other options could be considered by the 43rd president and 107th Congress:

- Index the DOD budget topline to a fixed share of GDP. Under current law, FY 2002 will be the final year of spending limits, or dollar caps, for the discretionary activities of the federal budget. This budget category includes DOD programs.[1] In July 1999 the CBO forecast that the share of the federal budget allocated to discretionary programs is expected to decline slightly from 32 percent in FY 2001 to 29 percent in FY 2009.[2] A key assumption for projecting federal budget surpluses for each fiscal year during FY 2001–2009 and for determining the overall size of the defense budget is that budget outlays for discretionary programs are expected to grow no faster than the annual inflation rate: If inflation is higher in nondefense programs, the defense budget topline must drop; if the defense budget is held constant and inflation is higher in DOD, DOD purchasing power will suffer. Thus, indexation would provide a mechanism for assuring some growth in the defense budget topline.

To accomplish indexation, the White House, DOD, and Congress must forge a new consensus and develop an action plan that is realistic about future military requirements and spending demands. This also will require an agreement among all three parties about the basis for determining future DOD budget levels. Historical long-term cost trends, as presented and discussed in chapter 3, clearly demonstrate defense costs grow faster than inflation, owing primarily to the demand for new, technologically sophisticated weapon systems and the annualized costs of acquiring and supporting them. Unless these historical cost trends are altered soon, defense budget toplines based on the discretionary program inflation average will result in lower DOD purchasing power over the long run. This in turn will lead eventually to smaller inventories of equipment for U.S. military forces.

■ Reduce further the active-duty personnel end strengths; savings could then be used to fund procurement of military equipment. Personnel cuts could include
  • 150,000 from additional force structure;
  • 60,000 from closure of 148 DOD facilities and bases (the United States would be left with 250 major domestic bases, roughly 50 percent of Cold War levels);[3]
  • 150,000 from outsourced work or reductions in DOD support missions.[4]

Figure 5.1 also illustrates the combined effects on force modernization of a reduction from 1.37 million to 1 million active-duty personnel under DOD budget levels indexed to 2.5 percent and 3.0 percent of GDP during FY 2001–2010. DOD spending levels indexed to 2.5 percent of GDP coupled with savings from a reduction from 1.37 million to 1 million in active-duty personnel end strength (circle d) would restore procurement spending to a level that would modernize and replace 54 percent of the QDR force. The same manpower cuts coupled with a DOD budget indexed to 3 percent of GDP (circle c) would increase procurement spending to a level that would modernize and replace 76 percent of the QDR force.

Thus, decisions on overall DOD budget levels and the number of active-duty personnel will determine the spending available for future force modernization. Force modernization in turn will define the size and technological sophistication of future U.S. military capabilities. Without procurement dollars, old military equipment cannot be replaced and new military equipment cannot be fielded. Military capabilities will deteriorate and eventually become lost forever.

WHAT TO BUY?

The second key action for the 43rd president and the 107th Congress must be to decide on what force will replace the QDR force. This is a decision about both timing and affordability. It is further complicated by the uncertainty about the nature of future military threats.

Timing of Defense Purchases

The need for early action by the 43rd president derives from the fact that the QDR force is running out of useful life and must be replaced. Unless new action is taken to extend or preserve the useful life of the QDR force, it will lose most of its current capabilities in the FY 2005–2015 time frame because of military equipment retirements and the absence of timely replacement units.

The urgency for action is best illustrated in figure 5.2, which provides in notional terms U.S. military procurement for three cycles or generations. Annual procurement spending is shown in this figure as a percentage of the total replacement value.[5] Most of the QDR force today is composed of military equipment that was procured in the late 1970s and the 1980s; the peak year of funding occurred in FY 1985, as in figure 5.2. The expected operational life of the QDR force today is currently estimated to be approximately 28 years; that is, the equipment of the force must be replaced on average every 28 years. Timely replacement of the QDR force would require a new procurement cycle commencing in FY 2000 with peak funding occurring in FY 2013; the procurement cycle would end in FY 2021. A third procurement cycle would commence in FY 2028, assuming no change in the service life of the military equipment. Peak funding would occur in FY 2041, and this third cycle would end in FY 2049.

A number of proponents, both inside and outside the Pentagon, are recommending that DOD accelerate military developments that would lead to an RMA force. For example, the 1997 NDP concluded:

> [W]e believe the United States must undertake a broad transformation of its military and national security structures, operational concepts and equipment, and the Department of Defense's key

Figure 5.2
DOD Procurement Cycles

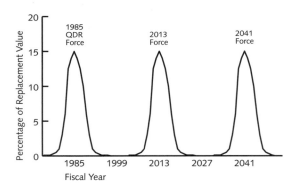

Source: MSTI estimates.

business processes. We recognize that much is already being done in this regard and that you are committed to significant change. However, based on our deliberations, it is our view that the pace of this change must be accelerated.[6]

This procurement strategy also is very attractive to those who believe that if the RMA force could be accelerated by 10 to 15 years it might be possible to skip the second—the middle—procurement cycle (FY 2000–2028), as shown in figure 5.3. Such a strategy would save badly needed dollars to pay for the development and acquisition costs for the RMA force and further ensure that the RMA force is adequately funded and brought to fruition—especially during an extended period of small procurement budgets as projected by the 1997 QDR.

Acceleration of the acquisition of the RMA force, however, does not address the near-term problem for the 43rd president and the 107th Congress: that is, the QDR force is running out of useful life, and it may happen during or immediately after their terms in office. In retrospect, senior defense officials in the 1990s paid perhaps too much attention to the RMA and future vision statements (FY 2028–2049) and not enough attention to the middle period (FY 2000–2028) in terms of what would be needed to maintain and sustain military capabilities.

Figure 5.3
DOD Procurement Cycles — RMA Force Accelerated

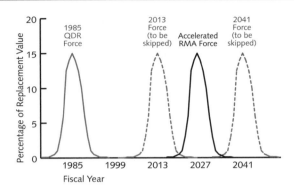

Source: MSTI estimates.

It now appears that the military services are starting to worry about the middle period. They started a number of programs in FY 1997 and FY 1998 to understand better their operational vulnerabilities or deficiencies during the middle period and to extend operational life of critical assets. For example, the air force increased the number of aircraft durability assessments and damage tolerance assessments, updated force structural maintenance plans, and enhanced or initiated aircraft tracking programs. The navy initiated a number of sustainment readiness programs (e.g., P-3) as well as remanufacturing programs (e.g., AV-8 and AH/UH-1) that effectively will extend the useful lives of critical assets. The army started in FY 1998 a life-extension program for its aging CH-47 Chinook cargo helicopter.

Three questions of strategy still remain, however.

- Are these recent programs enough to carry the QDR force through to the RMA force or are additional life-extending programs needed? Are additional programs affordable?
- What force structure and acquisition options are available to the military services if the RMA slips?
- Is this a cost-effective strategy for maintaining the technological lead in U.S.-fielded military capabilities?

It is important to understand that acceleration of the force acquisition cycle is a huge endeavor. The United States should exercise considerable caution before it embarks on such a course, which would involve in this instance the close synchronization of three major DOD efforts that were designed and organized to accomplish three separate objectives:

- Accelerate acquisition of RMA forces;
- Extend life of critical QDR-force assets for bridging to the RMA force; and
- Divest and restructure DOD infrastructure, support services, and business practices to pay for force modernization.

Equally important, this strategy must be carried out under the conditions of no visible threats, flat or declining annual defense budgets, and no technical failures. At the same time, for each of the three major DOD efforts, all of the traditional large-scale engineering, technical, and program-management risks must be identified and resolved: technical/ schedule, readiness, financial, and force integration.

Senior defense officials must overcome two major challenges related to the acceleration of the RMA force. The first management challenge will be to identify and provide funding and other defense resources for specific programs and activities that will transition RMA concepts to RMA forces:

- Establish requirements;
- Formulate concepts of operations;
- Define organizational units in terms of people, bases, equipment, and logistics support;
- Develop acquisition strategy;
- Manage acquisition programs; and
- Train and integrate RMA units into the total joint force.

The second management challenge will be to define and undertake those activities that will lead to large-scale changes in DOD organizations and processes; this is the conceptual heart of the RMA.

At the same time, in terms of extending the life of the QDR force, senior defense officials must determine and establish specific policies,

programs, and activities that will provide for the continuation of capabilities or services during the transition period, including

- additional new procurement programs such as life-extension programs, production restarts, remanufacturing programs, and
  increased purchases of commercial products and services;
- changes in peacetime and training operations and/or inventory
  management practices designed to conserve useful life of military
  equipment; and
- mitigation measures to counter and offset diminished effectiveness
  and nonavailability of equipment due to aging.

In terms of divesting and restructuring DOD infrastructure, senior
defense officials must be more aggressive and bold in their efforts to
streamline DOD support services and business practices and alter their
cost structure. Most important, they must be realistic about estimating
cost savings, focused and disciplined in program execution, and organized to harvest cost savings aggressively so as to ensure timely
payments for force modernization.

Finally, the success criteria for this course of action must be that the
capabilities of the RMA force will offer equal or better effectiveness
when compared with the capabilities of the QDR force today. It also
must involve less manpower, operate from fewer bases, be supported
easily and cheaply, and—most important—be affordable to acquire, operate, and support.

Affordability of DOD Purchases

Affordability will also be an important consideration of the 43rd president and 107th Congress in deciding what force will replace the QDR
force. As illustrated in figures 5.4 and 5.5, the demand of alternative
QDR acquisition programs for procurement dollars will exceed by far
the likely supply by at least a 2:1 ratio during FY 2001–2010.

With annual DOD spending limited to $266 billion, the 1997 QDR
estimated that annual DOD procurement budgets therefore are likely to
range from $47 billion in the worst case to $63 billion in the best case.[7]
Defense budgets in the $47–63 billion range also are well below what
was actually spent—$91 billion on annualized basis—to acquire the

Figure 5.4
Annual DOD Procurement Funding Options, Supply
FY 2001–2010

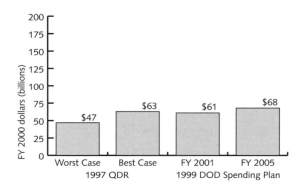

Source: MSTI estimates.

military equipment that makes up the QDR force today, as shown in figure 5.5.

The annual DOD procurement budget demands for various levels of modernization and replacement of the QDR force during FY 2001–2010 are

- $121 billion needed just to rebuy the QDR force at today's prices and technology products (e.g., F-16-C/D, F/A-18-E/F, DDG-51, M1 tank). This corresponds to the annual depreciation cost of the QDR force as shown in figure 3.5. The primary objective of this option would be the maintenance of current military capabilities for an extended period of time until the magnitude and nature of future threats are better understood and defense acquisition strategies and programs are adopted and implemented. Current QDR size, structure, and age are maintained under this procurement option. Procurement emphasis would be placed on force replacement.

- $164 billion needed to modernize the QDR force to the performance levels of planned next-generation military equipment (e.g., JSF, DD-21). This estimate reflects the current DOD practice of replacing older weapon systems with newer and more technologically

Figure 5.5
Annual DOD Procurement Funding Options, Demand
FY 2001–2010

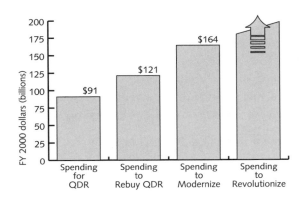

Source: MSTI estimates.

sophisticated and better performing weapon systems. Current QDR force size, structure, age, and technological lead are maintained under this option. Procurement emphasis is on force modernization and replacement.

■ more than $164 billion needed to acquire RMA capabilities. It is currently not possible to estimate procurement costs for this option because of the absence of consensus about specific military hardware to be developed and fielded for an RMA. Because of the emphasis on revolutionary technologies, it is assumed that procurement costs for this option would be higher than costs for only a modernized force. Size and structure of the RMA force would be very different from the QDR force; technological lead would be maintained or possibly expanded.

Whatever the technical merits of each of the three procurement options, not even the least expensive is affordable with defense procurement budgets in the $47–63 billion range or if we assume a procurement budget of $68 billion (the current DOD projection for FY 2005). Without an increase in the defense topline, the military services will have no choice but to reduce force structure and personnel levels.

New DOD acquisition strategy and programs therefore are needed. They must

- assign a higher resource priority to measures that extend and stretch the service life of critical military capabilities during the transition period so as to ensure availability to national command authorities (NCA); and
- define the speed at which future force modernization should proceed; that is, define the kind of improvement in capabilities that are affordable and represent the best use of defense dollars.

Finally, as shown in figure 5.5, DOD procurement budgets would have to average $121 billion over the FY 2001–2010 decade to rebuy the QDR force and its unmatched military power. With or without RMA, defense budgets in the $47–63 billion range strongly suggest diminished military power in the future. A smaller force would be inevitable, and the capabilities of this smaller force would be both different and fewer. What is not known today is whether this new force—being smaller and possessing limited reach—would be capable of carrying out the national military strategy and safeguarding and protecting U.S. national security interests and objectives in the future.

Notes

1 The Deficit Control Act of 1985 established spending limits, or dollar caps, for both budget authority and budget outlays for all discretionary budget programs. For FY 1999, the Deficit Control Act of 1985 specified three separate dollar caps for discretionary programs: defense, violent crime reduction, and nondefense programs. The number of separate dollar caps will fall to two in FY 2000 as defense programs are combined with nondefense programs. There will be only one dollar cap for all discretionary programs in FY 2001 and FY 2002 and no dollar caps beyond FY 2002.

2 The share of the federal budget allocated to entitlement spending is expected to increase from 56 percent in FY 2000 to 68 percent in FY 2009, while the share allocated for net interest payments is expected to fall from 12 percent in FY 2000 to 3 percent in FY 2009.

3 This estimate is based on a ratio that 20,000 active-duty personnel are eliminated for each 10 percent reduction in base structure. DOD reported a

total of 39,800 military and 70,969 civilian positions were eliminated as a result of the four BRAC rounds, which reduced the number of DOD bases and facilities by 20 percent. A 30 percent reduction in DOD physical plant therefore would eliminate 60,000 active-duty personnel and 212,907 civilian positions. See Cohen, *Report of the Department of Defense on Base Realignment and Closure*, 48.

4 This action would be consistent with the NDP recommendation that commercial-oriented tasks in the military be performed by personnel whose positions have been competed, that is, bid on for possible outsourcing. See NDP, *Transforming Defense*, 83.

5 The working assumption in figures 5.2 and 5.3 is that there is no cost growth from one generation to the next; hence the funding peaks would be equal. In reality, the actual amplitude of each successive procurement cycle will be higher than the previous cycle because of additional costs of technologies and better performance capabilities.

6 NDP, *Transforming Defense*, i.

7 This represents the 1997 QDR estimates that were expressed in constant FY 1997 dollars of $45 billion and $60 billion; $47 billion and $63 billion are the same amounts expressed in constant FY 2000 dollars.

CHAPTER SIX

CONCLUSIONS

CSIS EXPERTS HAVE WARNED SINCE 1995 OF AN UPCOMING DEFENSE TRAIN WRECK in which U.S. military forces and capabilities decline and deteriorate to a degree that the United States is de facto demobilized and possesses a diminished capacity to shape and influence world events and safeguard and protect U.S. national interests in the future. The defense train wreck would occur because, like the BUR force before it, the current QDR force is not affordable at the budget levels projected by the Clinton administration over the next 20 years (FY 2001–2020).

We reach this conclusion by comparing the funding needed to support fully the QDR force (demand for funds) with the funding that will be available (supply of funds) over the same period. This comparison has revealed that DOD will be faced with a budget shortfall of $88 billion in FY 2001 and of $573 billion during FY 2001–2005. We also estimate that the costs of fully supporting the QDR force will require annual defense budgets equal to 4.0 percent of GDP during FY 2001–2020, a 20-year period. In contrast, the Clinton administration projects that annual defense budgets will grow at an annual rate of 1 percent over the next decade, from $270 billion in FY 2000 to $293 billion in FY 2009. Thereafter, if DOD budget levels continue to grow at an annual rate of 1 percent during FY 2010–2020, the overall DOD budget will reach $327 billion by FY 2020. Given a growing economy, the defense budget will fall from 2.9 percent of GDP in FY 2000 to 2.4 percent of GDP in FY 2010 and to 2.0 percent of GDP in FY 2020. The budget shortfall will grow accordingly, from 0.9 percent of GDP in FY 2000 to 1.6 percent of GDP in FY 2010 and to 2.3 percent of GDP in FY 2020.

There is also growing evidence that future budget levels currently projected by the Clinton administration on the basis of its long-range vision for the nation and budget priorities might not be large enough to pay for

- developing and acquiring an RMA force within the next 25 years; or
- buying the next generation of military equipment needed to modernize the QDR force; or
- rebuying the current QDR force and military capabilities.

Thus the failure of the Clinton administration and the Congress during the past seven years to strike a new balance among strategy, forces, and budgets and the prospect that little will change between today and the next presidential election mean future presidents and congresses will have less time to implement solutions and likely will have to pay more for those solutions.

Although certainly welcome, President Clinton's budget proposal in February 1999 to increase defense spending by $4 billion in FY 2000 and $80 billion during FY 2000–2005, if enacted, may be too little, too late.

Until August–September 1998, senior U.S. defense officials for five years strongly rejected and denied any suggestion that defense plans were underfunded or not affordable. But today some senior DOD officials talk about a defense death spiral and nose dive. Their proposed solutions and priorities suggest, however, they are not fully aware of the extent of the defense budget shortfall. These statements coupled with the absence of significant progress as the decade of the 1990s comes to a close raise new worries that the defense train wreck may now occur earlier than previously thought—perhaps sometime during FY 2002–2007.

SIX INESCAPABLE FACTS

■ Higher DOD budgets are needed.

The inescapable fact is that in terms of maintaining and sustaining the military capabilities of the QDR force—the desired force for FY 1997–2015—DOD is facing budget shortfalls of at least $100 billion per year instead of in the range of $5–$25 billion. Until the White House, DOD, Congress, and the American public recognize and accept the magnitude of this financial problem and undertake specific actions to resolve it, the burden imposed on future presidents and congresses will grow heavier. Furthermore, the projected DOD budget shortfall is now large enough to raise serious questions about credibility and viability of the QDR force—even with today's optimistic budget assumptions.

■ U.S. military forces are entering a new period of vulnerability.

The QDR force today is composed of military equipment that was procured largely in the 1970s and 1980s. This equipment must be replaced on average every 28 years given its projected service life. Now, in the late 1990s, 20 to 25 years have passed since the start of the most recent procurement modernization cycle, and the QDR force is reaching the end of its useful life.

The average age of all air force aircraft (active and reserve) will be 20 years in FY 2000, well above the steady state average age of 15 years; this will rise to 28 years by FY 2010. At the same time, the average age of all navy ships and submarines will be 15 years in FY 2000 and will rise to 18 years by FY 2010—just below the steady state age of 19 years. The breadth and depth of force aging is further seen by the fact that 6 out of 10 major DOD combat weapon classes[1] already will be near, or well in excess of, their estimated service half-lives in FY 2002. In addition, the aging of the QDR force will undoubtedly lead to unexpected equipment performance and reliability problems that will require immediate action and dollars to remedy. The remedies will come at the expense of DOD procurement accounts.

During this new period of vulnerability, senior defense officials will be gradually compelled to decide on force replacement and modernization programs primarily on the bases of delivery time and the relative maximum benefit derived from the use of scarce procurement dollars. Near-term operational considerations will take precedence over long-term considerations. Without procurement dollars to purchase replacements, senior officials will have no choice but to accept reductions in QDR force capabilities at the moment the end of useful life is reached.

■ DOD O&S costs will continue to grow during FY 2001–2010 and will increasingly squeeze DOD procurement accounts.

For at least the next decade, DOD spending plans and budgets should be developed on the basis of continuing growth of O&S costs. Acceptance of this assumption would lead to the development of more realistic cost appraisals of current and alternative defense strategies, force structures, and acquisition programs. From FY 1960 to FY 1999, DOD O&S costs measured on a per capita basis for active-duty personnel grew at an annual rate of 1.6 percent. This cost trend has not varied since 1993 despite concerted efforts by the Clinton administration to reduce and limit O&S cost growth. In fact, DOD O&S spending per capita accelerated slightly under the Clinton administration—from 1.4 percent a year to 1.6 percent a year. Further acceleration of the cost trend is now likely as repair and maintenance costs escalate because of aging equipment and, eventually, programs that are undertaken to halt and then reverse the effects of the underfunding of defense in the 1990s.

As a consequence of continuing growth in DOD O&S costs, future military spending plans that seek to maintain a constant budget topline or a constant O&S budget share will at the same time need to identify measures for generating additional cost savings equal to, at least, the O&S cost growth rate of 1.6 percent per year. Failure will lead to the continuation of the DOD practice of procurement-dollar migration to O&S accounts to restore funding that was omitted owing to chronic underestimating of DOD O&S costs. This squeezing of the procurement accounts will lead to cutbacks or deferrals of planned procurement. The military services will add the deferred purchases to the future procurement bow wave. At the same time, procurement unit costs will likely increase further.

Without growth in the overall DOD budget, the O&S cost trend indicates that, by FY 2023, the O&S budget will grow to equal the entire FY 2001 DOD budget of $280 billion. This prospect in turn underscores the growing necessity and urgency for action today that will lead to, and will achieve in time, major reductions in the physical plant of DOD military bases and installations and a fundamental transformation of the cost basis of DOD infrastructure services. Therefore current efforts to create a revolution in business affairs within DOD must over the long run be structured and organized for determining measures on a continuous basis that will generate and increase savings equal at least to the current O&S growth rate.

■ DOD is facing a substantial acquisition challenge.

Future budget demands exceed proposed budget levels by at least a 2:1 ratio. The estimated annual demands for procurement dollars for three QDR acquisition program alternatives during FY 2001–2010 are

- $121 billion to rebuy the QDR force at today's prices and available technology products (e.g., F-16-C/D, F/A-18-E/F, DDG-51, M1 tank) at today's prices;[2]
- $164 billion to modernize the QDR force to the performance levels and costs of planned next-generation military equipment (e.g., JSF, DD-21);[3] or
- more than $164 billion to acquire RMA capabilities. It is currently not possible to estimate procurement costs for this option because of the absence of consensus about the specific military hardware that would be developed and fielded for an RMA.[4]

If total annual DOD spending is limited to $266 billion, the 1997 QDR estimates that annual DOD procurement budgets are likely to range from $47 billion in the worst case to $63 billion in the best case.[5]

Whatever the technical merits of each acquisition alternative, none of the alternatives is affordable with defense procurement budgets in the $47–63 billion range. The president's latest military spending plan raises the DOD procurement budget to only $68 billion by FY 2005. Without larger defense budgets, the military services will have no choice but to reduce both force structure and personnel and accept higher military risks.

Finally, defense budgets in the $47–63 billion range are well below what was actually spent—$91 billion on annualized basis—to acquire the military equipment that composes the QDR force today. Thus, given this range of spending, smaller forces are inevitable.

■ New DOD acquisition goals are needed.

The 43rd president and 107th Congress will have to decide which forces and capabilities will replace current U.S. military forces and capabilities. These major decisions must be shaped and formulated by a new DOD force modernization strategy and acquisition program that must define and specify the timing, technology character, and composition of the force that will replace the QDR force. The president and Congress also must address equipment aging and retirement issues owing to the fact that much equipment is reaching the end of its operational service life. At a minimum, the new acquisition strategy and programs must

- assign a higher resource priority to measures that extend and stretch the service life of critical military capabilities during the transition period to ensure availability to the NCA; and
- define the speed at which future force modernization should proceed; that is, define the improvement in capabilities that is affordable and represents the best use of defense dollars.

The new DOD force modernization strategy and acquisition program must be affordable over the long run and based on realistic assessments of defense costs and likely availability of adequate defense budgets. The new acquisition strategy and programs must refocus and energize DOD efforts (from the military laboratories to the operational units) regarding what is needed and when as well as how to leverage fully and continuously the scarce defense resources.

■ Additional force structure reductions are likely.

Without larger defense budgets and significant reductions in O&S costs, the military services will have no choice but make large force structure and personnel reductions. The new force might be smaller, older, and possibly less capable—especially if performance capabilities are minimized to meet cost goals. For example, an overall DOD budget that is maintained at 2.5 percent of GDP and structured to support an active-duty end strength of 1.37 million would leave enough procurement dollars to modernize and replace only 29 percent of the QDR force. Unless ways are found to extend the service life of military equipment, inventories must decline:

- DOD aviation forces (all services, both active and reserve) could decline from 15,578 aircraft to 4,659 aircraft;
- Navy ship and submarine forces could decline from 304 to 89;
- Army tracked combat vehicles could decline from 41,553 to 12,107.

Force structure or inventory reductions of this magnitude cannot sustain the current national security strategy or an ambitious foreign policy agenda.

POLICY CHOICES

The American public must better understand what it will cost for the United States to be a great power in the twenty-first century and must decide whether it is able and willing to pay those costs.

A major strategic challenge facing today's national security policymakers and decisionmakers in both the executive and legislative branches is the creation of a greater awareness and understanding of defense economics. All three defense strategy–budget reviews conducted in the 1990s suffered and lost institutional and public support because of participants' failure to understand fully and respond to the cost consequences of their decisions and recommendations. The DOD is soon to repeat the mistake as it prepares for the QDR of 2001.

The three strategy–budget reviews were driven largely by the politics of defense in terms of shaping and influencing strategy, forces, programs, and budget decisions. At some point, as senior DOD military and civilian officials are now discovering, fiscal realities must be confronted and resolved. Because greater consideration was not given to the economics of defense, the 1997 QDR, first, failed to recognize that the demand for future defense spending would exceed $266 billion annually and, second, failed to make the hard program choices necessitated by a decision to limit defense spending to less than $266 billion annually.

The danger therefore is that today we are likely to underestimate, not overestimate, the costs for our national security in the twenty-first century. We may believe tomorrow's national interests are protected but discover that we have failed to make the necessary payments between now and then. This is especially worrisome as current DOD budget pro-

jections show defense spending declining as a percentage of GDP—
from 2.9 percent in FY 2000 to 2.0 percent in FY 2020.

The year 2001 is emerging as a historic opportunity: the 43rd president and 107th Congress represent one of the last opportunities for
defining the military forces and capabilities the United States will possess by FY 2010 and the possibilities for the second decade of the coming
century. Bold and decisive action will be needed to avert the coming defense train wreck.

Notes

1 Combat weapon classes include strategic bombers, strategic airlift, air
force attack/fighter aircraft, navy/marine corps attack/fighter aircraft, attack
submarines, surface combatant ships, amphibious assault ships, Apache helicopters, Abrams main battle tanks, and Bradley fighting vehicles.

2 The primary objective of this option would be the maintenance of current military capabilities for an extended period until the magnitude and
nature of future threats are better understood and defense acquisition strategies and programs are adopted and implemented. Current QDR size,
structure, and age are maintained under this procurement option. Procurement emphasis would be placed on force replacement.

3 This estimate reflects the current DOD practice of replacing older
weapon systems with newer, more technologically sophisticated, and better
performing weapon systems. Current QDR force size, structure, age, and
technological lead are maintained under this alternative. Procurement emphasis is on force modernization and replacement.

4 Because of the emphasis on revolutionary technologies, it is assumed
that procurement costs for an RMA would be higher than for only a modernized force. Size and structure of the RMA force would be very different
from the QDR force; technological lead would be maintained or possibly expanded.

5 These figures are the constant FY 1997–dollar QDR estimates re-
expressed in constant FY 2000 dollars.

APPENDIX

ACRONYMS

AC	active component
APC	armored personnel carrier
ARG	amphibious ready group
AURC	average unit replacement cost
AWACS	airborne warning and control system
BRAC	base realignment and closure
BUR	bottom-up review
CVBG	carrier battle group
DOD	Department of Defense
DSB	Defense Science Board
ES	end strength
FTE	full-time equivalent
FV	fighting vehicle
FWE	fighter wing–equivalent
GDP	gross domestic product
HD	high demand
JSF	joint strike fighter
JSTARS	joint surveillance target attack radar system
LD	low density
NCA	national command authorities
NDP	National Defense Panel
O&M	operation and maintenance
O&S	operation and support (includes O&M, family housing, and military construction)

OOTW	operations other than war
OPTEMPO	operating tempo
OSD	Office of the Secretary of Defense
QDR	quadrennial defense review
R&D	research and development
RC	reserve component
RDT&E	research, development, test, and evaluation
RMA	revolution in military affairs
SSBN	ballistic missile submarine
SSN	attack submarine
TCV	tracked combat vehicle
UAV	unmanned aerial vehicle
V/STOL	vertical- and short-takeoff and landing
WOCV	weapons and other combat vehicles

INDEX

Page numbers followed by f, t, and n refer to figures, tables, and endnotes respectively.

Base capacity: excess of, 48–54, 52t, 53t; *vs.* manpower, in Bush and Clinton administrations, 48–49, 49f. *See also* Base realignment and closure (BRAC); Infrastructure

Base force plan, and Clinton, 23–24

Base realignment and closure (BRAC), 47, 48, 50–54; DOD procedure for, 64n–65n. *See also* Base capacity; Infrastructure

Bosnia, cost of, and FY 2000 budget, 7

Bottom-up review (BUR) of 1993: and Army National Guard readiness combat brigades, 42; and budget demands, 1; Clinton and, 23, 40; force structure results of, 23, 37–42, 41t; and regional conflicts, 26

BRAC. *See* Base realignment and closure

Bradley fighting vehicles, average age of, 32, 33t

Budget, U.S.: and competition for funding, 68–73, 69f; defense spending in, 3–6; emergency defense funding, 7; impact of Social Security on, 9, 25, 68, 69f, 70–72, 83; projected on-budget surpluses, 95n; and readiness, 4–6. *See also* Defense budget; Defense budget shortfalls

BUR. *See* Bottom-up review (BUR) of 1993

Bush administration: changes in force structure, 41t; defense budgets *vs.* Clinton administration, 54–55, 55t; and downsizing of military, 48–49, 49f; manpower levels in, 47t

CBO. *See* Congressional Budget Office

Center for Strategic and International Studies (CSIS), 1995 report. *See Defense in the 1990s: Avoiding the Train Wreck* (1995)

Cheney, Dick, on threats to U.S. interests, 26

Civilian pay: and budget shortfalls, 78–79; FY 1980–2005 trends in, 57, 58f; and inflation, 60t; *vs.* O&S spending, 77f, 78

Clinton administration: and base force plan, 23–24; and bottom-up review (BUR) of 1993, 23, 40; and BRAC process, 54; changes in force structure, 41t; defense budgets, 2, 3–4, 7–9, 54–55, 55t, 80–83, 124–125, 127; defense legacy of, 23–26; and downsizing of military, 48–49, 49f; and economy, 24; on force structure, 37–39, 42–48; manpower levels in, 47t; national security approach, 38–40; and O&S costs, 74, 76; and QDR 1997 force structure results, 42–48. *See also* Aspin, Les; Cohen, William S.

Cohen, William S.: on base closures, 51; on QDR 1997 force structure, 43; on quadrennial defense review, 1997, 3

Cold War, end of, and current threats to U.S. interests, 26–27

Combat vehicles, tracked: average age of, 32, 33t; budget-required force reductions in, 107–109, 107t, 108f, 130

Combat weapon classes, 131n

Congress: issues facing, 17–18, 110, 115, 119, 129; need for education in defense economics, 2, 130; view of military budget, 6–7

Economics of defense budget, importance of understanding, 2–3, 9, 130

Economy, U.S.: and defense budget, 54–56, 67–70; and defense spending in Clinton administration, 24; uncertain future of, 56–60. *See also* Gross domestic product (GDP)

Executive branch: issues facing, 17–18, 110, 115, 119, 129; need for defense economics education, 2, 130; view of defense budget, 7–9. *See also* Bush administration; Clinton administration

Fighter aircraft: average age of, 32, 33t; procurement cost growth, 90f; readiness of, 64n

Force, military, reluctance to use due to age, 18

Force characteristic recommendations of National Defense Panel, 92–93

Force structure: Aspin on, 38–39; balancing with defense budget, 111–114, 112f; budget-mandated reductions in, 101f, 102–109, 104f, 106f, 108f, 111–114, 112f, 126, 129–130; BUR 1993 and, 37–42, 42t; minimum floors on, 45–46; QDR 1997 and, 42–48, 126; reluctance to cut, 37–48; and technology *vs.* size, 34. *See also* Quadrennial defense review (QDR) force

Gansler, Jacques S., 5

Gross domestic product (GDP): indexing defense budget to, 113; projected growth in, long-term, 67–68. *See also* Economy, U.S.

Health care costs, increased, and O&S budget, 76

Inflation: and civilian pay, 60t; and defense budget, 59–60, 60t; and military pay, 60t; and O&M budget, 35, 60t; and procurement budget, 60t

Infrastructure: excess of, 48–54, 52t–53t; *vs.* manpower, in Bush and Clinton administrations, 48–49, 49f; size in FY 1997, 50. *See also* Base capacity; Base realignment and closure (BRAC)

Inside the Pentagon (journal), 63n

International Security (journal), 10

Johnson, Jay L., and overseas deployments, level of, 29

Krulak, Charles C., on cost of aging equipment, 35–36

Maintenance, and service life extension programs, 117–118; cost of, 36

Maintenance costs: of air force assets, 34–35; and budget shortfalls, 5, 14–15, 76; and defense industrial base, 36–37

Maintenance organizations, changes in, 36–37

Manpower levels: acquisition lead times and, 19t; in BUR 1993, 46, 47t; in QDR 1997, 46–48, 47t; reductions *vs.* infrastructure reduction, 48–49, 49f. *See also* Personnel

McCain, John: on overseas deployments, level of, 29, 30; on readiness, 6

Medicare: impact on budget, 69f, 70–72; projected shortfalls in, 71, 72–73; structure and financing of, 95n

Military missions, expansion of in Clinton administration, 23–24

Military pay: and budget shortfalls, 5, 14, 14f, 15f, 78–79; and FY 2000 budget, 7; and inflation, 60t; *vs.* O&S spending, 77f, 78; and recruiting and retention rates, 5; trends in, FY 1980–2005, 14, 14f, 15f, 56–57, 57f

Military retirement: and FY 2000 budget, 7; and Pentagon priorities, 5

Modernization cycles, and readiness, 16, 34, 115–118, 116f, 117f

National debt, impact on budget, 68–70, 69f

National Defense Panel (NDP), 1997: on base closings, 48; force characteristic recommendations, 92–93

National Research Council (NRC), Committee on Aging of U.S. Air Force Aircraft, 36–37

National security: Clinton administration approach to, 38–40; threats to, current, 26–28

Navy, average age of craft in, 32, 33t, 126

NDP. *See* National Defense Panel

1990s, defense legacy of, 23–26

NRC. *See* National Research Council

Nuclear submarines, procurement cost growth, 91f

O&M. *See* Operation and maintenance

Operational service life of equipment, and procurement levels, 88–89

Operation and maintenance (O&M): and inflation, 35, 60t; *vs.* O&S spending, 77f, 78; and

shortfalls in defense budget, 14, 14f, 15f

Operation and support (O&S): budget for, 127; budget shortfalls in, 73–80, 74t, 77f, 127–128; *vs.* O&M spending, 77f, 78; spending per of soldier, 74–75, 75f

Operations other than war (OOTW): effect on personnel, 30–31; expansion of, in Clinton administration, 24, 28–31; and readiness, 28–31

O&S. *See* Operation and support

Pay: civilian: and budget shortfalls, 78–79; FY 1980–2005 trends in, 57, 58f; and inflation, 60t; *vs.* O&S spending, 77f, 78; military: and budget shortfalls, 5, 14, 14f, 15f, 78–79; and FY 2000 budget, 7; and inflation, 60t; *vs.* O&S spending, 77f, 78; and recruiting and retention rates, 5; trends in, FY 1980–2005, 14, 14f, 15f, 56–57, 57f

PDM. *See* Aircraft programmed depot maintenance

Pensions, military, and defense budget, 5

Perry, William J., on defense budget, 81

Personnel: downsizing of, FY 1990–1999, 57; effect of operations other than war (OOTW) on, 30–31; readiness of, 28–31; recruiting and retention rates, 5, 6; reluctance to cut, 37–48. *See also* Manpower levels; Military pay; Military retirement

PL 105-33. *See* Balanced Budget Act (1997)

Power of U.S. military: and defense funding levels in Clinton administration, 24–25; increasing questions about, 18; limited life of, 16–17

President. *See* Executive branch

Prestige of U.S., and aging military force, 18

Procurement: cost of deferring, 100–102, 110t; efficacious timing of, 18–19, 19t, 115–119. *See also* Acquisition

Procurement budget: causes of inaccurate estimation in, 86–87; Congressional Budget Office (CBO) estimate of, 109n; force reductions needed to fit, 101f, 102–109, 104f, 106f, 108f, 126; funding levels for, 83, 88, 120–122, 120f, 121f; funding shortfalls in, 13, 14f, 76, 83–94; FY 1980–2005 trends in, 58, 58f; implementation times for, 18–19, 19t, 115–119; and inflation, 59, 60t; *Report of the Quadrennial Defense Review* (1997) on, 83–85; required level of, 99; shortfalls in, 99–109, 100t; and unit-cost growth rates, 89–94, 90f, 91f

Procurement cycles: extension of, 117–119, 117f; projected, 115–116, 116f

Project Air Force, on aging of equipment, 34–35

Public, and defense economics, need for education in, 2, 130

Quadrennial defense review (QDR) 1997: and age of equipment, 33–34; and budget for 1999, 3–4; and budget shortfalls, 84, 99–100, 124; and defense funding, reconciling strategy and budget, 2–3; and fiscal reality, recognition of, 2–3; force structure alternatives, 43t, 44–46, 44f, 79–80, 79t; force

structure results, 42–48; manpower levels in, 46–48, 47t; and regional conflicts, 26. *See also Report of the Quadrennial Defense Review* (1997)

Quadrennial defense review (QDR) force: challenges facing, 126; and Clinton administration, 23–24; current state of, 25–60; depreciation cost of, 88–89, 89f; funding levels required for, 99; funding of, 1–2, 9–17; replacement value of, 87–88, 87f; required replacement of, 115–119. *See also* Force structure

RAND Corp., Project Air Force, on aging of equipment, 34–35

Rapid deployment force, Clinton advocacy of, 38

RDT&E. *See* Research, development, test, and evaluation

Readiness: aging of U.S. forces and, 31–37; Congress and, 6–7; decline in, 4–6; of fighter aircraft, 64n; McCain on, 6; modernization cycles and, 16, 34, 115–118, 116f, 117f; operations other than war and, 28–31; of personnel, 28–31; Shelton on, 4

Recruiting and retention rates: fall in, 6; and military pay, 5

Regional conflicts, danger of, 26–27

Reimer, Dennis J., and overseas deployments, level of, 30

Replacement cost: of 1997 QDR force, 87–88, 87f; of aircraft, projected, 103t; of ships, projected, 105t; of submarines, projected, 105t; of tracked combat vehicles, projected, 107t

Report of the Quadrennial Defense Review (1997), 3, 43, 45, 81; on procurement budgets, 83–85. *See also* Quadrennial defense review (QDR) 1997

Research, development, test, and evaluation (RDT&E): and shortfalls in defense budget through FY 2005, 14f, 15f; time frame for, 18–19, 19t

Resource–strategy balance, method of attaining, 111–114, 112f

Retirement, military: and FY 2000 budget, 7; and Pentagon priorities, 5

Revolution in business affairs, DOD support of, 51, 115

Revolution in military affairs (RMA): capability requirements for, 119; DOD support of, 51; funding of, 1; likelihood of achieving, 92, 125; overemphasis on, 115–117; and procurement costs, 92, 93–94, 115–119, 117f

Right-sizing of U.S. forces, as Clinton motto, 39

RMA. *See* Revolution in military affairs

Ryan, Michael E., and overseas deployments, level of, 30

Service life extension programs (SLEP): cost of, 36; and procurement cycles, 117–118

Shelton, Henry H.: on budget shortfalls, 6, 14; on deployment frequency, 14; on force readiness, 4; on military pay, 57

Ships, U.S.: average age of, 32, 33t, 126; budget-required force reductions in, 105–107, 105t, 106f, 130

Short-notice deployments, impact of, 30–31

Size of military force, minimum floors on, 45–46

SLEP. *See* Service life extension programs

Smaller-scale contingency operations. *See* Operations other than war

Social Security: impact on budget, 9, 25, 68, 69f, 70–72, 83; projected shortfalls in, 71–72, 72–73; structure and financing of, 95n

Strategic airlift assets, average age of, 32, 33t

Strategic bombers, average age of, 32, 33t

Strategy–budget balance, method of attaining, 111–114, 112f

Strategy–budget reviews (DOD), and recognition of cost consequences, 2–3

Submarines: attack, average age of, 32, 33t, 126; nuclear, procurement cost growth, 91f

Technology, *vs.* force size, 34

Threats to U.S. interests: *Annual Report to the President and the Congress* on, 26–28; current, 26–28; lack of, 5

Training, for operations other than war (OOTW), effect on personnel, 30–31

Unit-cost increases, and procurement budget, 89–94, 90f, 91f, 103t, 105t, 107t

United Nations rapid deployment force, Clinton advocacy of, 38

ABOUT THE AUTHORS

DANIEL GOURÉ is deputy director of the CSIS International Security Program. Gouré joined CSIS in April 1993 following two years in the Office of the Secretary of Defense as director of the Office of Strategic Competitiveness. He has been a defense analyst with System Planning Corporation, R&D Associates, Science Application Corporation, and SRS Technologies, and has published widely in such journals as *Orbis*, *Comparative Studies*, and *Military Technology*. He holds a Ph.D. from the Johns Hopkins University and has taught there and at the National War College, Air War College, Naval War College, and Naval Postgraduate School.

JEFFREY M. RANNEY is director for strategic planning and financial analysis at Management Support Technology, Inc. (MSTI) in Fairfax, Virginia, and a senior associate at CSIS. Ranney is a nationally recognized expert in defense budget forecasting, strategic planning, and defense economics and has presented defense budget forecasts to senior civilian and military leaders. Before joining MSTI, he was a member of, and later managed, the long-range defense planning consulting practice at System Planning Corporation. He holds an M.A. from the Johns Hopkins University and has coauthored articles in *International Security* and *Armed Forces Journal International*.